The Bearded Doctor

The Bearded Doctor

Stories of a Medical Officer
in Northern Nigeria
1953-1963

DR MICHAEL McALISTER HOLMES

BROWN
DOG
BOOKS

Published under licence by Brown Dog Books and
The Self-Publishing Partnership, 7 Green Park Station, Bath BA1 1JB

www.selfpublishingpartnership.co.uk

ISBN printed book: 978-1-78545-310-6
ISBN e-book: 978-1-78545-311-3

Written by Michael McAlister Holmes
Compiled by Ruth and Alison Holmes
Edited by Erica Rolfe

Cover design by Kevin Rylands from a design by Alison and Ruth Holmes
Internal design by Andrew Easton

Printed and bound in the UK

FOREWORD

Professor Alison Holmes FMedSci
London, 2018

These are just some of a collection of true stories that my father, Dr Michael McAlister Holmes, wrote about his experiences as a senior medical officer in Nigeria in the 1950s and early 60s, a time of great transition and turmoil for the country and a time of much learning about endemic diseases. He left Northern Ireland as a young man, to serve as a doctor and medical officer in Nigeria, spending almost fifteen years there, working hard, with colleagues he greatly admired, and gaining increasing responsibility and seniority. He also earned enormous respect for his medical and surgical skills, expertise, commitment, his training of staff, developing teams and running hospitals and health services, as well as for his kindness, compassion and humour. He loved the country, felt privileged to work with such great colleagues and was very sad to leave, always wishing to return someday.

These stories and observations were originally typed up by him on his old typewriter in the heat on scraps of paper, some written later, when we were living in Tanzania, after leaving Nigeria. He wanted to record some of the incredible and unique experiences that he had, working as a medical officer there and at that time. Some are personal stories, many filled with humour, some are tragic, while others address *medical and political* mysteries; all written with his keen eye and warmth.

I was born in Northern Nigeria in the 60s, in Yola. My brother Thomas had been born three years earlier in Belfast as, for the birth of her first child, my mother went back to Northern Ireland by ship. Two years after my birth, the family left Nigeria for good, with great sadness. My father could never settle in Britain after his years in Nigeria; he found the medicine less interesting and challenging, and missed the outdoors, the environment and the people. Although he worked a while in Ireland, he could not settle down there so went on to work in Tanzania, Yemen, Libya and then Swaziland, places we all lived together as a family.

My father was a great diagnostician with extraordinary powers of observation, and a forensic ability to swiftly identify constellations of subtle physical signs and syndromes.

As well as being well known as an excellent and kind physician, he had a reputation for as a talented surgeon, working in very challenging circumstances. A large part of his work and responsibility was in public health, to which he was deeply committed. Addressing women and children's health, planned parenthood and ensuring the provision of safe and supportive maternity services was always a major focus of his attention. He also had a great interest in preventing and interrupting the transmission of infectious diseases, as well as their individual management. He developed a wealth of experience in this field and bore witness to the huge impact of endemic infections, outbreaks, epidemics and emerging diseases. He also knew an enormous amount about the management of venomous poisoning, having to deal frequently with snake and scorpion bites.

He avidly kept up with the literature and advances in medicine no matter where he was in the world, devoting time to reading and correspondence.

Outside his work he had a deep love for the African bush which he shared with us, along with a keen interest in the flora and fauna, including insects. He enjoyed solitude when he could grab it and carried the weight of enormous confidences. He also enjoyed company, getting on well with diverse groups and individuals and was always very sociable. He was a great man for a party and a great dancer, but was also famous for managing to slip off early! Above all, he was a devoted father and husband.

While working in Swaziland my father developed pancreatic cancer and died when he was only 56, working until shortly before he died. I was a second-year medical student at Cambridge at the time, and was profoundly shaken by his death. I had been blessed with having been so loved and supported by a great father and being in such a stable family unit, with such a strong sense of home, wherever we were in the world. Over the years there have of course been many times in my life when I longed for him to be there at significant occasions, milestones and celebrations, and I continue to miss all the warmth and laughter. Missing my father has been a constant backdrop to my career in medicine, particularly in my field of infectious diseases, with a recurring feeling of loss every time I wanted to chat to him about all the interesting things and medical advances that I know would just fascinate him; I would still love to hear his thoughts.

My mother Ruth, now in her nineties, has worked tirelessly on this book. She had her own professional life in Nigeria, serving as a teacher in secondary education and in developing access to secondary education, frequently the only woman in her working environment. As we worked together to collate these stories and images, I came to understand even more the extraordinary life she led in Nigeria and her strength, love and humour in supporting my father in his role, even though there was much he could not share. As you read the Sultan's story, keep in mind that she knew nothing of his visits to the Sultan's palace: my father could not share any of this with her at the time.

Thanks from us both to Erica Rolfe, dearest friend since our families lived and worked in the Yemen in the early 70s. As her family also spent time in Nigeria in the 60s, she was able to edit these stories with a gentle hand.

Dad left a tantalising list of titles of stories (overleaf) typed up, that he never got around to completing. These range from the management of cancrum oris in leprosy, and the early recognition of Burkitt's lymphoma to the bravery of a man injured by a train, to stories of touring by camel, of fishing experiences and fish festivals; and what was the 'Ilorin goat killer' all about? Nevertheless, I hope the following stories give you a flavour of his time in Northern Nigeria, his dedication, humour, and his love for the country and its people.

Dr Michael Holmes drawn by Belfast artist George Morrison (his brother-in-law)

The Sultan's leg or the Policeman's baby.(Circuits, theatre table, surgical drums and the different routes to palace.

His Head was not correct. Police case, back to front.

The £5 French Corset story - ?change.

Snake juju - garden protection. Snake smell. Juju to make one invisible to snake or hyena or people etc.

The No Children Tribe.

The Perfect Murder - Mushroom -liver toxins plus juju - to die on a certain day.

Muckovey ducks eating toads.

3½ years woman like an animal, husband in for life attempted murder and her recovery en route to another hospital.

The Bobbing Baby Alive - Mammy wagon overturning 50 drowned in fadama accident.

Camping in S.Yola thunder storm -Fire balls, boiling water lightening. (Kortishi rocks?)

Rail injuries- Ist. Fulani boy hitch hiking on train-ticket collector-jumped -R.foot. 15mls.

2.Ca stomach in hospital cured by juju.

3. Convulsion treatment for infants -cooking them in front of fire!

4. Baby feeding with gruel by cupped hands.

5. Cancrum oris (removal of maxilla in in girl whose Ma was a leper.

6. Kwashiokor.

7. The now Burkitts' tumour.

8. Rabies, small girl, man in Sokoto hosp barking etc. Cat, Donkey and dog rabies Catering Rest House world wide information

9. Pea-nut deaths from inhalation (sigmoidoscope).

10. Leprosy clinics cases walking 10 or 15 miles to and fro for Dapsone + *Antabuse?*

II. 4gallons hydrocele - man fainted then walked home!

12. Bladder stone on 13 yr old boy.

13. Fibulectomy on girl 15 yrs.

14. Rag and bottle plus cahter for head and neck operations with funnel.

Stories that were never written

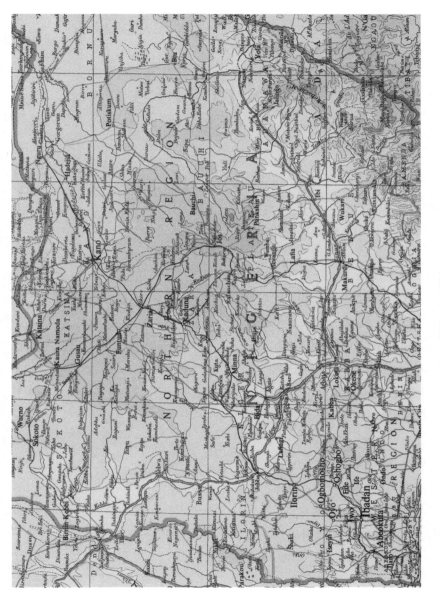

Map of Nigeria 1956

11

CONTENTS

IN THE MOOD FOR ADVENTURE

Ruth Holmes

It wasn't long after Queen's Elizabeth's Coronation on 2 June 1953 that Michael set sail for Africa.

We had married at the end of 1950 and had both worked in Belfast during the intervening months.

Michael qualified as a doctor at Queen's University Belfast in 1950 and spent a few months studying for his DRCOG (Obstetrics and Gynaecology), before working as an assistant in a busy city practice.

I had met Michael at university and since graduating, I had been teaching in a tough secondary modern in Belfast. He often worked late into the night and I always made a very early start in the morning to cross the city to my school.

We had rejected the offer of his father's practice in Wales and had turned down the idea of a practice in a rich farming area in County Armagh or one in Leicester. 'Too far away from the sea,' I remember saying. Little did I know how far from the sea we would end up.

As students at the end of the Second World War our travelling had been limited to cycling in Ireland. We were in the mood for travel, for adventure and the challenges ahead. So Michael set sail for Lagos and I flew out a short time later.

Michael had been given the name of a Colonial Service man who had lived in Nigeria in the 1940s and met up with him in London. This chap had a scar across his face, the result of a mauling by a leopard! All the way up to Kaduna by train for hundreds of miles Mike was on the lookout for wildlife. He saw nothing at all and neither did we when we travelled together from Lagos some years later. We found out, however, that the man with the scar was the only person in the Colonial Service ever known to have been attacked by a leopard.

Mike and Ruth Holmes

1.

DEPARTURE

1953, Liverpool

The grey hulk of the *Accra* was towering above me as I finished with the luggage checks in the cold Liverpool warehouse. The covered gangplank was a blessing as the cold rain poured down. Along the upper decks the ship's officers and crew were lined up, taking a look at the new cargo of bodies who would be their charges for the next twelve days or so. In the ship's foyer were heaps of luggage arranged roughly according to cabin number. The stewards yelled out B48, C243, D560 etc and the owners shouted 'here' or 'me' until the stewards picked up the cases and showed the owners to their cabins.

My steward, John, was an elderly man from the Wirral and was full of the 'Yes, sir, your first trip to the west coast?' 'A Doctor of Medicine, yes', 'White man's grave, very hot and sticky'. He hastened to add, 'You soon get used to it!' I took stock of the cabin which had its own bathroom and porthole; my berth was the inner one. My cabin mate arrived, Bert, a weedy chap with glasses, who had the appearance of either a brilliant physicist or a nutcase. Like me, it was his first trip to the tropics of Africa.

There was still pandemonium in the foyer as people struggled to find and claim their cases so Bert and I went to get afternoon tea. The dining room was full of our fellow passengers, and with friends and relations saying tearful goodbyes. The klaxon sounded for all visitors to proceed ashore. The ship's staff were running up and down the corridors, passengers and friends in groups, lost children in duffel coats bawling. The klaxon blared out the second warning to visitors to proceed ashore, derricks whirred, tugs hooted, hammers banged on the stay boltsof the ships' doors and there was a bustle of activity until the gangway was finally lowered. Then came the piped music, tear-jerker stuff to make you wonder if it was wise to embark on this trip. Everyone lined the rails waving to those on land, a little band of devoted missionaries going out for at least five years to the African bush, tears welling with both happiness and sorrow; for many of them it would be the last time they would ever see their folk who stood on the quayside; they choked and sang hymns and we all joined in.

The National Anthem was piped as the ship eased herself off the dockside; it was the moment of truth. Most of us were on the verge of tears or choking back the emotion, with thoughts of dear ones and the life left behind. A popular dance tune and the sound of the ship's hooter as we edged away from the docks brought us all back to the present. Friends and dockers gradually faded away and we watched the tall Unilever tower recede into the pall of smog as we entered the Irish Sea.

Elder Dempster ship

I began to take stock of the passengers on my first voyage to Africa, all herded together for the next fortnight. There were the colonial types, tall, rakish men with weather-beaten faces, loud-mouthed and with a military bearing. Smoking cigars or cigarettes in long cigarette holders, sporting colourful cravats or old school ties. Well-worn suede desert boots would flap the decks as they walked in their peculiar superior manner. Their wives, too, were often tall with wrinkled faces, and long necks sporting the black thread of their lorgnettes, with heavily made-up lips, gold rings clustered with rubies and diamonds over their well-worn hands, flat chests and penetrating voices.

Their husbands usually had one droopy lower eyelid from the constant popping in and out of monocles. They would walk together around the decks, talking loudly of stocks and shares, trips to Paris or their boy at Eton or Harrow.

Then there were the younger 'sports', in their flashy clothes, gay socks and flapping sports coats, laughing heartily and eying the younger married wives and unattached girls.

Then there were the 'boozers', a heterogeneous crowd of men of every shape, size and age with one common denominator, to drink as if their lives depended on it. The ship's bar was open each morning from seven o'clock to eight o'clock and there they were, tousled hair, bleary eyes, wearing their warm woollen dressing gowns or raincoats, slouching into the bar in bedroom slippers or gym shoes, knocking back double rums, whisky or gin in a wraith of tobacco smoke. They hardly spoke to one another but once suitably fortified, left en masse at eight cheerily calling 'see you at twelve'. They then disappeared to their cabins not to be seen again until midday when the bar reopened and they had slept, shaved and looked a bit more presentable for the lunchtime session, which went on until two. One or two of them staggered in for lunch but usually they were not seen until just before six, hanging around the bar until it opened and staying there until midnight. They had their own 'pitch'; they never mixed with anyone and they never appeared to be drunk and disorderly. At the eight am session they would be joined by the 'colonial' types having their double 'pinkers' to start the day.

Others such as the missionaries seemed to wish to be on their own, to walk around the decks, read, write letters, or stare at the sea. They were constantly badgered by the sporty types, trying to coerce everyone into playing competitions: deck tennis or cricket, quoits or table tennis. Other couples kept coming around for money, running daily run bets; in fact we were pestered all the time.

During the first few days at sea we could sit anywhere in the dining lounge except at the captain's table, with the purser, first engineer and ship's doctor. The greasy head waiter put up the table seating chart on a blackboard at door of the dining hall. Certain 'honoured' guests' names were allocated seats on the ship's officer table, so everyone knew who they were. It was then panic stations for the young sporting types desperate to sit with their own crowd. The head waiter then just assigned the rest of us chair numbers and there you had to stay for the rest of the voyage.

On my right I had Bert, and in front of me a sea captain who was joining a ship on the West African coast. Our other companion was a labourer who was going to work on some building site; everything was 'effing' this or fu_ _ that. These two were attached to the 'boozers' and often missed meals. Our table was right at the far end of the dining hall and from my seat I could see most of the other people and also see out of the porthole above our table. After twenty-four hours I knew it would be impossible for me to get on with Bert, who argued with everything or proved his point by mathematics. The sea captain caught him out several times and eventually the rest of us talked among ourselves and ignored Bert.

There was always drama at the 'cage', a structure on the upper deck where babies and toddlers could be put while their parents went for their meals or to the bar. It was supervised by a large woman, known to everyone as 'Nurse'. Her job was an unenviable one; most of the kids appeared to hate her guts. When Mum or Dad tried to leave their children with her, they bawled and kicked and often had to be manhandled into the 'cage' where they would scream and shout, clinging onto the wire with tears rolling down their cheeks.

The weather was now getting appreciably warmer and the skies bluer, and the sea became calm and flat. The swimming pool was now opened on the upper deck and white, hairy legs, sandals and colourful shirts appeared on the men, suncream, pink noses, coloured glasses and various patterned, billowy robes covered the ladies over their bikinis and bathing costumes. Chilled drinks with straws were everywhere and spilt ice cream melted on the decks. The cold air blowers were going full blast and sweat poured as we walked between one blower and the next. The crew donned white shirts, shorts and white stockings, but their shirts or tunics were always soaking wet; some even carried a small towel on their shoulder just to mop themselves.

There was great excitement when a shoal of porpoises appeared gambolling around the vessel, their dorsal fins cutting through the water, then jumping high into the air. With the intense sun and glare from the sea, flat as a vast mirror, there came a kind of euphoria. More screams and excitement as hundreds of jellyfish, the Portuguese man-of-war, sailed past in the shimmering sea. We soon got blasé and did not even bother to get up to peer over the side.

I was trying desperately to read up about tropical diseases that I might encounter but found it hard enough to say, never mind spell, some of the horrifying diseases: trypanosomiasis, schistosomiasis, dracunculiasis, and all the permutations of the malaria parasite. It felt like every insect or creepy-crawly harboured plague, yellow fever or some hideous rotting skin disease, depicted in gruesome detail in the black and white photographs. I began to wonder how anyone could stay alive in the tropics, where water, food and even people carried so many ghastly infectious diseases.

Trying to remember such drugs for treatment was another nightmare: Chenopodium oil for certain worm infestation of the bowels, chaulmoogra oil an old treatment of leprosy, tryparsamide, pentamidine or suramin for sleeping sickness, tartar emetic and stibophen for bilharzia, the host of drugs for the prevention or prophylaxis of malaria, plus the various quinine derivatives for the cure of malaria. Banocide™ for filariasis which causes elephantiasis and for another horrible worm that causes blindness; Onchocerca volvulus and for another that causes Calabar swelling or Loa loa.[1]

It was like attempting to learn a new language, and filled me with misgivings. I was constantly interrupted to partner other passengers to play table tennis, deck quoits or deck tennis. Fortunately I only got through to the second round of table tennis.

Africa at last

The engines stopped while it was still dark; we had arrived at Freetown estuary. On deck, it was stiflingly hot and humid and I was drenched in sweat. The air was thick with swirling mist and it was hard to catch your breath. Through the patches of steam coming off the sea small dugout canoes appeared, manned by skilful young boys shouting at the passengers to throw down sixpences. They would spin out of their frail craft and dive into

---

1 These were the drugs being used in the 1940s and 50s. Some are no longer used as they were toxic and had side-effects, or have been replaced by more effective and safer alternatives. However, some are still used today.

the sea and retrieve the coins with a cheery 'Thank you, messa'. As the sun rose the mist gradually disappeared: my first sight of Africa!

The ship anchored in the middle of the large estuary of the river which could be discerned disappearing into the forest of trees and palms. On the headlands were the large, white coastguard buildings and along the banks of the river were the colonial houses, surrounded by greenery of various trees and lush grasses. At the estuary entrance was an old shipwreck, a reminder of the last war; I wondered about the appalling conditions that our troops must have suffered with the heat and glare of the place and the ever-present worry of what was lurking under the surface.

I could not help remembering the etched pictures of Freetown in old school history books of the slave trade: little was changed except for a number of newer houses that had sprung up along the coastline. The ship's derricks clattered away, lowering cargo onto the barges that had come alongside. Those passengers who were leaving the ship, and even their motor cars, were lowered over the side. By now there were many dugouts, some brimming with pineapples and other fruit, coconuts and gaudy cloth. The barges ferried backwards and forwards all day long and later a few passengers came on-board, camping on the after deck with their mats, pots and pans and colourful robes and dresses. The oppressive heat and humidity were overpowering and I wondered how I would manage in this hothouse atmosphere.

Later that day we drew up anchor; the small boys were still diving for money but now their price was two shillings or two shillings and sixpence. If a sixpence or threepenny bit was thrown they would ignore it. On the bottom of their dugouts were piles of silver and coppers. How they managed their small skiffs, jumping in and out all day, constantly bailing them with coconut shells, being stung all over by jellyfish, no food – it was a hard way of making money. As the ship drew away they paddled frantically to meet the large waves that it generated bow on – paddling, scooping, waving, with tuneful 'bye-byes' and 'see you again'.

The athletic types were getting into their stride, second or third round of games being played as if their very lives depended on it.

By now the passengers each had their own 'deckchair' places, seats in the library corners in the bar, or certain tables that they 'booked' by leaving a handbag or cigarettes and lighter. The children in the 'cage' were now quieter and the Galahads had chummed up with the nurse, as her charges were more amenable. Then came the day for the Finals, with the betting types now putting on private wagers, and everyone turned out to watch the spectacle, except the boozers of course. While we watched, several groups were going around to see who would enter for the swimming gala – diving for plastic rings, blind man's bluff and the slippery pole pillow fight.

Passengers and children crowded around the small swimming pool with water sloshing from side to side as the ship rolled. The ship's younger officers were the organisers. Proud mothers and fathers watched their youngsters dive for the rings: those who picked up the most from the bottom of the pool would get a prize and the competition was keen. The same for blind man's bluff, where the person who managed to duck his or her opponent's head under the water was declared the winner.

The climax of the gala was the slippery pole. Four bronzed and tattooed seamen appeared and placed the pole across the pool. They then produced buckets and long-handled, angulated paintbrushes. They liberally slathered the pole with soapy, greasy liquid from the buckets. The kids went first: most of them never even made it to the centre of the pole, it was diabolically slippery. Some tried to clear the pole with the pillow, but jiggling along to get rid of the grease did not work. Others took a swing just as they reached the centre but they, too, toppled into the pool.

The following day we crossed the Equator and so another afternoon at the pool with the traditional ceremony for those crossing the line for the first time. Father Neptune arrived with trident, funny hat and a massively long beard that reached to the deck. A chair was placed near the pool edge and Father Neptune and his helpers liberally doused the cheeks with outsized brushes with soapy, greasy stuff and then attempted to shave it off with an enormous razor made from three-ply wood. Everyone was splattered with soap and then pushed into the pool, then towards the end Father Neptune and his helpers were themselves doused with the contents from the buckets by the first-timers.

Takoradi, Ghana, was our next port of call, where a few passengers disembarked. It was quite an extraordinary port, just along the coast with no piers or bunds, the ship simply manoeuvred itself alongside the quay. I was struck by the greenery and the lovely Flame-of-the-Forest trees. The Gold Coast people with their shiny, coffee-brown skins and the gaudily coloured robes and headgear were truly startling. I was intoxicated by the contrasting colours. The ship took on a number of deck passengers and a big canvas awning was hoisted aloft to give them shelter from the sun and rain. Compared with Freetown, the atmosphere was much clearer, hot but not so humid. There were frequent heavy showers, but as soon as the rain stopped the sun came out and everything appeared dry and clear again.

We were nearly at the end of the sea voyage and a sort of apathy affected the passengers who became quiet and subdued. The daily gambling game of guessing the mileage that the ship had done in the last twenty-four hours seemed to have lost its appeal.

2.

ARRIVAL AT THE PORT OF LAGOS

Everyone was up early packing their trunks and cases, landing papers completed, passport and health cards ready. Boxes in the hold were claimed and stacked up in separate piles. Derricks clanked as they lifted up the hold covers. The ship's crew worked frantically to change the dining room into offices, the Library Bar closed up, and everyone was scurrying about. The ship's engines were down to half-revs as we slowly progressed over the bar into the Niger estuary.

On the shore we could see ornate houses and gardens, the Governor's residence with the Union Jack flying, his private jetty and launch. Then the Yacht Club with boats of different colours and shapes. The greenness was not nearly as striking as in Takoradi. It started to rain. I had never seen such a deluge: within seconds the decks were flooded and water sloshed all over the place. This only lasted a short while and soon everything was steaming again.

As we docked there were hundreds of dock labourers waiting to start work, with jet-black bodies, and some just wearing loincloths. As the gangway went down, officials surged aboard: police, Customs, bankers, health personnel. Then came relatives and friends to meet the passengers. Government and business representatives shepherded the passengers to form queues at the various temporary offices that had been set up on-board. Eventually we struggled down the gangway for the last time, as porters carried massive cases and trunks on their heads down to the Customs Shed to be claimed.

The shed was a large barn affair with a tin-pan roof and the heat inside was stifling. Around the side were big letters, A-B, C-D etc, where the porters placed all the baggage according to surname. It was organised pandemonium and tempers were short, exacerbated by the extreme heat of the place. I had two shotguns and ammunition for game so I had to go to a special counter to get entry permits for them. I also had a very pleasant Nigerian Customs Officer checking the rest of my luggage. I nearly went into a panic as I could not spot the last chap I had spoken with in the sea of new faces. I had to open one box: there were no tools or hammers, but fortunately it was not too hard to open. One Dutch passenger had all his possessions packed into lovely, wooden barrels. They were not numbered and he had to open all of them to find the one where he had packed his rifle ammunition. He spoke very little English and he was drenched in sweat as he tried to open his barrels with broken bits of packing case timber. He was the last one out of the Customs Shed!

Eventually we were all sorted out and I took my hand luggage and guns into a minibus along with other passengers, and we were dumped at the Ikoyi Hotel. The hotel porters efficiently collected our respective loads and took us to our rooms. Again I had this awful feeling of wondering if I would ever recognise all these new faces.

I shared a room with another passenger from the ship to whom I had spoken only a few times. The room was very dark and had mosquito netting over the windows and doors and a clanking ceiling fan that swished the hot air around. The room had a peculiar musty smell from the growth of fungus in the cracks and corners. The bathroom was across the main corridor. The hotel bar was well stocked with every conceivable drink and the barman was a rotund, cheery man who spoke at least half a dozen languages and could mix a good cocktail.

I had a look outside and was amazed by the colour, the Flame-of-the-Forest trees, the violet flowers of the jacaranda, the pink lilies and the bright green leaves. Ants were everywhere. Suddenly I saw a lizard scurrying by, with its yellowish red head and blue body. It gave me quite a shock to see the much duller-coloured female lizards. There was no shortage of food for them: they lay beside an ant trail and just ate their fill as the ants passed. I was amazed to see vultures at the rubbish area, so tame you could almost touch them. Long, curved beaks, beady, blinking eyes, red, S-shaped necks, dull brownish-black feathers hopping on scraggy legs from one morsel to another or slowly flapping their wings to sail into the air.

The traders outside the hotel were fantastic; mostly Northerners wearing small, white skullcaps over their shaved skulls and coloured, flowing robes. Sturdy Raleigh bicycles were everywhere, with large tyres and carriers piled high with cases, and bows, quivers and arrows suspended from the handlebars. The traders were selling plumes of feathers, brightly coloured leather poufs, handbags made from snake, crocodile skins, long coils of dried-up python skin, cowhide drums of every shape and size, locally made flip-flops from skins and even old car tyres. Everything had been put to a good use, even old bottles and cigarette tins had been beautifully covered in coloured leathers. Polished cow horns had been carved into animal shapes or shoehorns or back scratchers, ebony carved heads or masks, tables, wooden ornaments, were all for sale.

Lagos to Kaduna

I had two nights in the hotel and then was taken to the main railway station to catch a train for the two-day journey to Kaduna. My crates and wooden boxes were all neatly piled up on the platform. These were checked and then the porters loaded them into the luggage compartment. The passenger compartment was for four people: each of us had a corner seat. One bench seat had a door in the middle, through which were our toilet, washbasin and shower. All the windows had an outside window that you could pull up and down, and on the inside a mosquito net that you could raise and lower, as well as a blind to keep out the sun. Above us was a small fan that oscillated back and forwards, whirring around the hot air.

We settled into this new environment and unpacked our toiletries. One of my companions was going all the way to Port

Harcourt by train, which would take him three to four days; another, a British Army lieutenant, was going only a short way, while the third was going to Kaduna like me. After what seemed like ages the guard's whistle went, the train made steam and hooted and we slowly drew out of the station. I was excited and looking forward to seeing the animals of tropical Africa and my eyes were glued to the windows so as not to miss sighting any game. The train gradually gathered momentum as we passed through the shanty outskirts of Lagos. Then we were over bridges nearly all the time as we crossed the swampy ground of the estuary and suddenly entered the mangrove swamps. The tree canopy got thicker and higher as we entered the tropical forest belt.

Now we travelled almost in darkness as the rail track wended through the enormous trees and lianas. Everything was green and vibrant with ferns growing out from the trees, and the undergrowth was covered in high grass with narrow paths winding through dark passages. I kept looking, hoping to see colourful parrots or monkeys or more, even a leopard or other wild animal, but apart from the horrible vultures at the various stops I saw absolutely no game or wildlife.

At regular intervals, the steward would inform us that lunch, supper or tea was ready and we would walk along the passageway through a couple of coaches to the dining car. We seemed to pick up fresh fruit as the train went along and I remember the delicious, small pink bananas: I have never had anything like them since. We seemed to stop at every clearing and halt when the various officers of the train would get out to meet friends and have a good yarn, then whistling and hooting, the train would groan and shake and we would be on our way again. The larger stops had platforms, but these halts had nothing except hundreds of hawkers selling food produce: eggs, live chickens, fruit, rice and corn cobs baked black over an open fire.

When we returned from our supper our compartment had been made up into a four-berth sleeping compartment. The seats and the recessed upper berths had been pulled out. Clean sheets, pillows and a heavy, Army-style blanket were laid on top, all neatly folded, edges nicely tucked in and the mosquito net blinds pulled down. The heat was stifling and the wee fan was just not big enough to be effective.

A nice veterinary couple I had met on the ship were also on the train. We exchanged books and papers, but I was mesmerised just looking out of the window, always expecting to see a wild animal, but I saw none the entire journey.

3.

KADUNA

I arrived in Kaduna by train and three or four hours late. There was a well-lit station and a wild cacophony of sound in many languages I had never heard of. Expatriates were either in groups or on their own, but I could not see anyone I recognised. I was just getting my gear out of the compartment, when a handsome Scotsman wearing a white, open-necked shirt, khaki shorts, long, white socks and brown brogues came up to me. 'You must be Dr Holmes, our new gynaecologist,' he said. 'My name is Bruce Nichol. Welcome to Kaduna.' I was swept off my feet from then on. He arranged the transfer of my luggage to a kit car, an open truck. He took me to the Catering Rest House in his enormous Chev motor. Speaking in Hausa, Bruce saw that I had a chalet to myself and instructed the staff to take good care of me. When I commented on his proficiency, he said he could not speak it as well as other Nigerian languages. He then left me saying he would call for me in an hour or so, when I would meet his wife Mary and have supper at their house.

I did some unpacking and the Rest House steward Shehu diligently hung up my suits and ran the bathwater and cleaned my shoes. I noticed the lizards, this time one was upside down on the ceiling – a gecko – an amazing creature slowly moving its tail from side to side like a cat when it is stalking. Suddenly it pounced, with a fly in its mouth.

Bruce drove me along a bumpy dirt road, with Flame-of-the-Forest trees lining the lovely drive up to his house. It was a 'Lugard-style' white house, with black-painted woodwork and tubs of roses on the verandah. I was astonished.

I had prepared for a life in the 'bush' in darkest Africa, bringing with me all sorts of canvas equipment. Instead I found an elegant mock-Tudor house with electricity, even an enormous ceiling fan inside, turning around in its cupola, which was filled with golf balls to stop the fan wobbling.

Bruce's wife Mary told me the roses were McGredy's roses from Portadown in Northern Ireland. Years later, I would look out upon acres of Northern Ireland roses once again from our home in County Down.

Lugard-Style House for Medical Officer, Kaduna

My first morning in Kaduna. Bruce collected me at seven o'clock and took me round the nursing home to introduce me to the Sisters and staff. The building was quite large, on two stories, with wide open verandahs on both levels and white-painted shutters. Next door was the Sisters' mess and their quarters.

About half a mile away was the Medical Headquarters for the Northern Region, housing the offices of the Director of Medical Services (DMS) and Deputy DMS, as well as the Finance and Personnel Departments. This was my first meeting with my new DMS, a stern character with a gruff manner. Later, I came to like him.

Bruce then took me down to the General Hospital, with its large red cross sign on a white and black background. The entrance gate had an archway of offices above it. The gateman let us in through the milling crowd, while on the verandah, a policeman controlled fairly orderly queues of pushing and bustling men, women and children. This, I was told, was the outpatients department.

Bruce was the physician in charge of the nursing home and the TB cases at the general hospital. He introduced me to my immediate boss, a Dr T, who was in charge of the general hospital. Dr T was one of the strangest characters I have ever met. He was of average height, round-shouldered with rather aquiline features, a beaky nose, a receding forehead and blue eyes. He always carried a floppy school satchel-type of briefcase. It went everywhere with him, but I only ever saw him take out his stethoscope. I never knew if there was anything else in it! He always wore a tie with his floppy shirt and his long trousers seemed too baggy. He had an incredibly quiet voice: often I could not catch what he was saying. When he spoke, his head would go back, eyes closing as if he were going into a trance, then suddenly they would open right up and peer at you. He was very fond of music and gave the impression he was perpetually listening to the strains of a faraway orchestra. He smoked in an odd way, holding the cigarette between his middle and ring finger. He had a great sense of humour and a fierce temper. He took some time to get to know, but he was a really decent man. He was extraordinarily helpful, giving me 'cogs' (reminder notes, guides) of the treatment of the various tropical diseases, all of which were new to me. As I learned that first day, there was absolutely no time to ask for assistance at the morning clinic: we had to see over 300 outpatients every morning before breakfast.

Outpatient queue

Arrow points to policeman with cap on. At this door we had fun and games with people trying to beat the queue!

On the office table were two bottles: one was filled with a long tapeworm, and the other was filled with what looked like earthworms, but were in fact roundworms, both common intestinal parasites. The patient would come in and say, 'I shit worms, Doctor'; we would point with a biro to each bottle, the patient would give a nod, and by then we would have written down the appropriate medicine and dosage.

Dr T took me round the various wards and made an operating list for me for the next day – simple stuff – a hydrocele (to break me in!) then two inguinal hernias, some suturing of old wounds and a couple of intramuscular abscesses. I nearly died at the thought. Apart from assisting at operations, my experience of operations consisted of one hernia under the supervision of an eminent surgeon in Belfast and carrying out a lower segment Caesarean section with a consultant surgeon overseeing. Now I was on my own!

The theatre staff were terrific. My anaesthetist was an elderly senior staff nurse whose equipment consisted of a trolley with a lot of small bottles covered in blue material and several metal face masks in various sizes. He induced with his own concoction of chloroform and ether. The patient began breathing in the stuff from the rag and bottle, and after a few coughs and splutters, all hands secured the patient on the operating table as the excitatory stage was reached, the thighs were strapped down and soon a sonorous breathing would be heard, as the patient went quietly asleep.

My assistant was the theatre supervisor, Patrick, an excellent man in every way, sympathetic, kindly, a skilled nurse and a first-class assistant. He helped me through the morning session of operations, my first taste of real surgery. We soon became a great team, relying on each other day and night.

During this first week in Kaduna I had to do one of the most challenging and memorable Caesarean sections of my career. Bruce called me in to see one of his patients, as he was concerned. She was a lady doctor, an elderly primigravida, with an extended breech presentation. My first obstetrical problem in Africa on a fellow doctor – what had I done to deserve this?

She was a great patient and later became a good friend, but I sweated blood at the time. External version was adopted but obviously failed at this late stage, as she was in the ninth month of pregnancy. A Caesarean was the only safe and wise thing to do – and it was down to me.

I scrubbed up, feeling sick: my bowels had turned to water. The soap was slippery and kept sliding out of my shaking hands. My assistant was to be Bruce Nichol and this time my anaesthetist was an Army brigadier, whom I had never even seen before. He arrived in his uniform, swagger stick, red braid everywhere and had a big, booming voice. He had brought along his own anaesthetic machine and the patient went under nice and quietly. I was gowned and gloved, and the patient was draped and surgically cleaned. Scalpel in hand, I asked the brigadier if the patient was ready. Then I began the operation, and all fear and nervousness left me.

Bruce assisted me well. He had not seen a lower segment operation done before, but he did everything I asked. A lusty baby was soon extracted and quick to cry. The midwife took care of the baby while I stitched up the mother, who was then taken by ambulance to the nursing home. Everything had gone off exceptionally well and everyone was happy. I was exhausted and happy to accept some refreshments from my new Scottish friends later that day.

Apart from the medical challenges in the clinics, hospitals and nursing homes, my first nights in Africa were a nightmare; I had the most dreadful diarrhoea. Every night it was the same, dead tired, crawling on my hands and knees to the toilet: after twenty or so times I would give up counting. Having to see a mob of outpatients, or sweat it out doing operations in the mornings in such a state, felt unbearable. I was ready to resign. Then suddenly the diarrhoea stopped.

A good thing, because soon after Dr T was posted and I found myself in charge of the General Hospital, and that was a whole new story.

Kaduna General Hospital Entrance

Kaduna Medical Staff

Kaduna Midwives and Nurses (Midwifery teaching models of a baby
and a pelvis displayed in front)

4.

MY FIRST TOUR INTO THE BUSH

I had been in Kaduna for only a few weeks when I was summoned by my senior medical officer to go to a village apparently stricken with meningitis. It was about 60 miles to a roadside village, then another two or three miles into the bush.

I had to leave straight away and get this checked and contained before a major outbreak of this killing disease swept the countryside, so I rushed home, collected my camp kit and got my cook steward, Gumbo, to get the 'chop' box ready with provisions for a couple of days.

The main road at this time was unsurfaced, just laterite, and as we drove the surface became more corrugated and bumpy. I skated along, sailing over the corrugations with no real control, just hoping not to hit such a big pothole that it would wreck the car.

Normally the journey should have taken about two hours, but neither Gumbo nor I had any maps and we did not know the roadside village, so we had to keep stopping at every hamlet or hut along the way, not to overshoot the place. After some hours we found the roadside village and I left Gumbo with the car, to set up quarters in the village hut, while the village head procured a guide and an English-speaking interpreter for me.

I was told that the villagers were dying in a small compound, about three miles into the bush, but that the paths were good and that the easiest way to get there was by bicycle. Out of nowhere three bicycles appeared and I selected the one with a sort of carrier over the back wheel, to which I lashed a Gordon's gin bottle filled with drinking water; it was coming up to noon and the sun was getting very hot. Over my back, I had a satchel, a bit like those used to carry service gas masks during the war. I filled it with Sulpha tablets, glass syringes, needles, cotton wool and disinfectant. Off we rode into the bush.

It did not take long to discover that my bicycle had seen better days: the wheels were eccentric, so even on the flattest surface I went up and down alarmingly. The saddle soon began to make an impression on my backside as the leather seat was worn down to the metal frame. It was soon agony to ride as my bottom got more painful and hot. I tried to ride the bike like a horse and rise up on the pedals every time I came to the 'corner' of the wheels but my legs soon gave out. After an hour of this, winding and twisting up and down hills and carrying the bike over small streams, I began to wonder if we would ever reach this hamlet. 'Just around that small hill there', was always the answer. The sweat was now lashing off me and I had finished my bottle of water. At last the village appeared: I was exhausted, my backside was raw and my legs were like rubber.

The hamlet was virtually empty, one or two people were wandering around in a trance. I began to look into the huts but at first could see nothing in the darkness. The buzz of flies and the smell were nauseating and as my eyes adjusted there on the floor were the dying and prostrate bodies, each with half a calabash of gruel beside them, lying in their own vomit and faeces.

There were about twenty huts, each with one or two bodies inside, some barely alive and others who had succumbed. A pervading stench and the pall of death hung over the hamlet. Vultures were circling overhead and some of the bolder ones were sitting on the grass roofs, occasionally flitting down to have a peep inside the huts. The inhabitants had left, taking their dogs and chickens with them, leaving only two people to give the dying their gruel or filthy water to drink.

I worked furiously, injecting the moribund and giving pile of Sulpha tablets to those who could swallow and to anyone who had been in contact with the cases. It was indeed meningitis[2] and I needed to speed back to get the Public Health Department sixty

---

2   Nigeria experiences widespread severe epidemics of cerebrospinal meningitis (CSM) causing many deaths, due to the transmission of the bacteria Neisseria meningitides. Geographically Nigeria sits within the 'meningitis belt' across Sub-Saharan Africa, where outbreaks occur in the dry season. The disease can rapidly be fatal if not treated with antibiotics promptly. In the 50s, unlike now, there were no vaccines available to prevent this disease and protect people, although antibiotic drugs were then available, and at that time these antibiotics were sulphonamides. Controlling it was based on case detection and verification, early treatment with antibiotic injections, isolation, and antibiotic tablets prophylaxis for contacts, surveillance and communication and coordination across the affected states. Nigeria continues to face these epidemics.

miles away to send their team as fast as possible to try to contain the disease and prevent a large-scale epidemic.

I sat on the crossbar of my bicycle (there was nowhere else) and tried to think if I had done everything I could do …. I had no words.

5.
MY COOK GUMBO

As well as accompanying me on medical tours Gumbo was also my cook. I first met him shortly after my arrival in Kaduna while I was still staying in the Rest House. Shehu, my chalet boy, came sauntering along to the verandah where I was sitting, followed by a big man wearing a red fez on top of his head. The man had on a long, white shirt which billowed out over his baggy, white trousers and he wore khaki-coloured gym shoes – Army issue.

His skin was very black and he had some attractive facial scarring, longish streaks down his sideburns. He had a large mouth with rather prominent teeth, stained by tobacco and cola nuts. He had a wonderful smile and his sparkling eyes were full of mischief. I took to him immediately.

Shehu introduced me to his friend and said, 'Gumbo is a very fine cook.' Gumbo came forward, shook his fist in greeting and then extended his right hand. 'Good evening, Sah', he said with a tremendous grin and his eyes sparkled brighter than ever as we shook hands. 'I be for Army before and been cook for many English people. Look, see my papers.' He then delved into his pockets and brought out many pieces of paper, some brown with age, some crumpled and others so folded that they fell to pieces. These were his references.

My cook Gumbo

I wish I had copied them out, as they were excellent at disguising what Gumbo was really like. 'Gumbo has been my cook for three years – dishes excellent. But one had to watch the market money' or 'Watch your spirits, especially your gin'. He was obviously a rogue, but a very likeable one. He was tough, too: he had been awarded a medal for bravery in the late West African Frontier Force, very handy on tour in the bush.

I employed him immediately as my cook, for the following day I was moving into my own bungalow. The kitchen was small and outside the house. There was a wood-burning Devon stove, which appeared to be pretty dilapidated, but the bread Gumbo made in it, including delicious rolls, was out of this world. His omelettes were terrible, like leather on the outside and frothy inside. I was just about getting used to them, when my wife arrived from UK. When she tasted Gumbo's omelettes, she exploded. Omelettes apart, his cooking was good and he would always excel himself when we were giving a dinner party, producing all the little extras that made the main course taste really good.

One of the best tips we got from him took me some time to understand. He wanted gin, preferably Gordon's, for the turkey. We bought our poultry live and it was the cook's job to prepare the birds. On one particular day I was home and wanted to see what he did with the Gordon's. We went outside and watched as Gumbo caught the turkey and wedged the bird's body between his legs. With its head in his left hand he opened its beak with his right and gradually poured a large glass of gin down its throat. The turkey did not seem to mind this, but soon the wobbly flesh on its neck went a peculiar dull red then blanched and became pale pink. The bird staggered around and Gumbo allowed it to do so for a few minutes and then he cut its throat in true Muslim fashion. The bird was completely relaxed and the meat after cooking was white and deliciously tender.

One evening we had some very special guests coming to dinner and my wife had told Gumbo what to make and what courses to serve. It was 7 o'clock and the guests were arriving at

7.30 pm, but Gumbo had not appeared. Ibrahim, the steward, had arranged the cushions, cigarettes, trays of nuts and glasses in the sitting room and the dining table had been laid, with flowers set in place and decoratively folded napkins. Everything was ready except the food.

I had bathed and was dressed in my white shirt with cummerbund and black bow tie, as well as my mosquito boots of lovely soft leather. My wife was all ready to change, her long evening dress on a hanger, but Gumbo still had not returned and she was in turmoil. She was upstairs looking out of the window and I was downstairs fortifying myself with a whisky and wondering what we were going to do, when Gumbo arrived at last.

When my wife heard him talking to the steward, she shouted at me to give him a good 'telling-off' and a threat of notice. I went over to the outside kitchen to admonish him and there he was with hot logs blazing on the fire and wearing his red fez over his shaven pate, a white apron over his bare chest and in his khaki gym shoes. The sweat was pouring down his face and shoulders, he looked as if he had just come out of a shower. On my entry he tried to stand to attention and managed to give me a very wobbly salute and shouted, 'Sah!' It was obvious he had been to a 'palm wine bar'. Palm wine was the local alcohol, made by draining sap from the palm trees and allowing it to ferment. When I saw Gumbo in front of the roaring fire, covered in sweat and with his fez at an angle and evidently inebriated, I just didn't have the heart to tell him off. I attempted: 'Ah Gumbo, you be late,' and he answered, 'Yes, Massa. I truly be sorry, but Memsahib's dinner will be fine too much, Sah.' I just couldn't control myself and burst out laughing and we both laughed and shook hands. I then told him quietly that Memsahib was very upset and please not to take so much palm wine before a dinner party in future. We parted on the best of terms.

Unfortunately, my wife had seen us from the bathroom and heard our conversation and our laughter. Now I was the one in trouble.

'What will dinner be like?' she asked furiously. Fortunately for me, in the middle of this tirade, our first guests arrived. I rushed to greet them and my wife came down cool and collected and full of smiles, as if nothing had happened. The steward served drinks, more guests arrived, introductions were made and I slipped out to the kitchen to see how Gumbo was progressing. The kitchen was like a furnace, the perspiration on him was like a shower, but the roast smelt lovely, as the gravy had been prepared with good stock and the vegetables were bubbling away. The evenly round bread rolls were ready and piping hot and the greenery for garnishing the dishes was all set out. Everything seemed under control and ready for when we wished to eat. I gave my wife the nod that everything was OK, the ladies retired and the men had one more quick drink.

My wife arranged the seating and then sat down, her heart in her mouth, wondering what was going to appear. First there was fruit, then soup, then the main course with vegetables including potatoes, then a dessert with various biscuits and cheeses and finally coffee and liqueurs.

It was a terrific meal, beautifully cooked and served, and I was partly exonerated.

We found Gumbo a good cook when he was sober. However, when he was drunk he was superb.

When we left we recommended Gumbo to our new Matron and heard many months later that she had arrived home one day after a bush tour and found Gumbo sleeping in her guest bed between her new sheets, wearing his red fez, old apron, khaki trousers and still in his Army-issue gym shoes.

On tour as Medical Officer, attending to patients in villages

6.

TWO CASES OF MALARIA

A telephone call from Medical Headquarters, followed by a confirmatory wire, 'DR BRUCE CHWATT ARRIVING THIS PM. VERY ILL. FOR IMMEDIATE ADMISSION'. Dr Chwatt was the Chief Malariologist[3] for Nigeria and his book 'Essential Malariology' was my bible on the disease! 'I put myself in your hands,' he said.

We admitted him and examined him and looked at a blood slide and it was indeed malaria. All that he wanted was to be better within two or three days, to continue his tight schedule of touring the villages. He was a great patient and we quickly had him back on his feet. He was soon able to continue his tour and went on to chair the 2nd Malaria Conference in Lagos in 1955.

---

3 The distinguished malariologist Leonard Jan Bruce-Chwatt (1907-89) headed up the Federal Malaria Service of Nigeria from 1949 to 1958. He then moved to Geneva to become Chief of Research and Technical Intelligence in the Malaria Eradication Division of the World Health Organization.

Not long after this I received a call from my SMO saying that a Polish doctor was motoring down with a patient who had become mad and violent. The doctor had to drive about 350-odd miles in his kit car over dirt roads with his patient. On that same day, I was expecting a visit from Professor Rogers, my Professor of Surgery at Queen's Belfast, who was coming to stay for a few days.

The doctor duly arrived with his 'mad' patient, Roy. I went to see him after he had been admitted to the nursing home. Roy was stockily built and was sitting beside his bed in a wicker chair, wearing his pyjamas and dressing gown. He was quiet and non-communicative, and looked surly. I left instructions regarding his treatment and let him settle into his new surroundings after the very long and tiring drive.

We had just welcomed Professor Rogers into our house and were sitting down chatting when the phone rang. It was the Sister in the nursing home requesting me to come quickly as the new patient was running about the home creating havoc. I took the Prof down to the nursing home with me, there was the patient walking down the stairs with the Nursing Sister and the Matron following about six steps behind, carrying a syringe in a kidney dish. His chest was bare and very hairy, and he waddled down onto the patio like a gorilla, with a venomous appearance.

The Prof and I were getting out of the car when he picked up the massive, wire-meshed shoe scraper and flung it at us like a skipping stone. I ducked and it very narrowly missed the Prof but hit the car. We escorted Roy to the prepared isolation ward downstairs and, with the aid of a couple of nurses and Matron, we bundled him into bed and gave him a deep intramuscular injection of a narcotic. In a few minutes he was fast asleep.

We all went upstairs to see the havoc he had caused, hurling fire sand buckets about the corridors as if they were ping-pong balls. The nursing staff had been afraid for their patients' lives, as there were maternity cases and some very serious medical cases in the nursing home at the time. The Sister had tried to cajole him, but once he began throwing the sand buckets about she was really afraid.

As Roy was such a large man I requested that two policemen be on permanent duty outside the isolation ward or 'cage', as we sometimes called it. I also told them to bring along handcuffs and leg irons in case he got really violent. It took me some time to get to the bottom of why Roy had become like this. Apparently for two weeks he had forgotten to take his mepacrine prophylaxis for malaria and, when he suddenly remembered, he took fourteen tablets at once. He did not feel too well following his overdose of mepacrine[4] and then went to see the Polish doctor who diagnosed malaria and promptly gave him at least two further doses of mepacrine!

---

4 Mepacrine was a drug used for the prophylaxis of malaria at that time; however, it was associated with many side-effects, and is no longer used. One of the side-effects was toxic psychosis.

7.

GOVERNMENT PRISON

One of my duties as a Colonial Medical Officer was the supervision of the local prison and the prisoners. There were some very distasteful aspects to this, such as supervising the flogging of the prisoners who had misbehaved, for example striking a prison warder.

One of the major problems in a large government prison in Northern Nigeria was to cater for all the various diets of the prisoners from such a vast and diverse country. Nigeria covers every type of geographical terrain, from the jungle forest and swamps in the south to the arid desert zones in the north and everything in between, from ravine, plateau, hill, to open savannah country.

Some prisoners ate only rice and fish, others only meat, others fruit and vegetables, many others followed religious laws – Muslims who would not eat pork or meat not killed in the proper fashion – or differing tribal beliefs.

One day the chief prison officer called me to his office which was situated over the main gates of the prison. On the front was the main road and the back window overlooked the prison yard with the various compounds: cell blocks, open-bucket latrine blocks, a work yard and a sealed-off section for the occupational therapy group, with weaving looms, basket making etc.

The chief was worried about the amount of money that he had to spend in getting fresh fish up from the south, oranges and limes from the mid-zone and the dried meat or biltong from the northern parts. He felt that if I thought that these prisoners were lacking in any vitamins, then fair enough, the government would pay for the extras, but if they were fit and not showing any sign of malnutrition or vitamin deficiency then they could go on the very adequate if monotonous prison food. I agreed to examine the 100 or so 'special diet' cases.

On the appointed day there was a neatly lined-up parade of prisoners outside the sickbay, about a dozen standing in a queue at the door while the rest were sitting in an orderly line on the prison yard.

Those standing at the door were the tough and strong men from the Cameroon delta area, all over six feet tall with a wonderful physique. Accompanied by the chief warder and several other warders who would act as interpreters, I entered the office and sat down at my desk. The first dozen strong, strapping men showed excellent teeth and healthy skin, and had maintained their weight since their arrival at the prison; some had even put on a few pounds.

So I indicated on their files that ordinary prison food was perfectly satisfactory for the first dozen, then the next and so on, all except for sixteen or so very old or sick prisoners.

As the examination progressed a gradual mumble outside the sickbay grew louder and louder, then all of a sudden, a wave of massive prisoners barged into the office, demanding that their special meals should be reinstated. They brushed past the warders, ready to pick me up and throw me over the prison wall. I was terrified. Eventually the warders were able to get them under control again. The chief warder called for the chief prison officer and, after some compromise, peace was restored.

The prison officer had a peculiar sense of humour. For minor offences or ridiculing of the prison warders or officers he had a nasty trick of getting the culprit to head-carry the latrine buckets, especially the rusty and leaking ones. This was a terrible punishment, as the latrine bucket gang had to march out of the prison to the night-soil grounds so everyone could see the prisoner being punished. If he was from the town, this was an especially humiliating experience for the offender, who would soon beg forgiveness.

The offender never knew when the chief would let him off this filthy and smelly job: it could last a few days or continue for weeks. He would be shunned by the other prisoners because he smelt and he could never get his prison garb rid of the foul odour. After a stint of this, the chief warder usually had a really well-behaved prisoner.

One of the pleasantest jobs as a prisoner was working in the sickbay: there was no hard work. The orderly organised the early morning clinics, cleaned and dusted and made up the four beds that we kept for mildly sick prisoners.

The sickbay orderly prisoner assigned at that time had a

withered right arm, possibly from a birth injury. He was a very pleasant chap, spoke good English as well as a number of other languages, and was really most helpful to me.

One day the chief prison officer came to visit me while I was working there and this unfortunate orderly made a two-finger sign behind his back, but the chief caught him out of the corner of his eye! As quick as a flash the chief had him marched off with two warders to the latrine lines to collect the rustiest bucket available. He joined the gang, head-carrying the bucket leaking like a garden hose out of the gates. I've rarely seen such misery and humiliation: he begged for a lighter bucket as he had only one good working arm, but to no avail. After he had been on this job for a few days he had an argument with the warder and tried to hit him, and the next time I saw the poor wretch he was in the condemned block.

The block was within the prison, surrounded by a high wall and a closed, solid iron gate, so once inside a prisoner could see nothing but the sky, ground, walls and the locked-up cells. It was a depressing place where prisoners were made to break up stones with a hammer into various sizes for building. The prisoners here had their feet shackled, and they used pieces of grass or string to hold up the chain between their feet as they shuffled about. Those condemned to the death row were also handcuffed and locked up most of the time.

My ex-medical orderly was there, legs shackled and wielding a mason's hammer with his good hand, belting stones. He scowled at me, but I could do nothing for him.

It was here that the prison held the monthly flogging of

prisoners who had been really bad: these were really vicious men capable of anything.

On the appointed day, the chief officer and warder would present a list of offenders. I would have to medically examine the listed prisoners on the morning of the flogging to make sure that they were fit and well. They were nearly always fit, but if for example a prisoner was suffering from an attack of malaria, punishment would be postponed. The district officer would often be in attendance: the warders on duty on these mornings were usually the tallest and the strongest ones.

The culprits were lined up on one side of the condemned cell block; a small trestle was in the middle of the yard. All the condemned prisoners, including the ex-orderly with the withered arms, were in a semicircle around the trestle. Leaning up against the wall were about three or four large bundles of sticks, about six to seven feet long and about three-quarters of an inch thick.

In the front of the queue were the Hausa: these were men who showed no fear or pain. At the end of the queue were the weaker ones, both mentally and physically. They would be the last ones to receive their floggings. The first man would be led by one of the enormous warders to the trestle, the prisoner then took off his shorts and bent over the trestle, his chest pressed on the top, and over his exposed buttocks the warder placed a square of surgical lint which was dampened with water.

The chief warder announced the number of strokes that the prisoner was going to get, usually six or twelve. He would then point to a warder who was to beat the prisoner. No warder knew whom he was going to flog or if he was going to be called to do the beatings or not. The selected warder then went and collected one of the long sticks, did a couple of swishes in the air to make sure it was pliable, then took aim on the piece of lint; bent the stick back over his right shoulder then took the other end in his left to bend the stick like a bow, then with an almighty swing with his right brought the stick down with all his strength. The stick would only last one or two whacks before it disintegrated, then another was picked up from the pile.

If the warder was able to make the prisoner shout he would be given an extra half-day off: this was to ensure that there was no favouritism, tribal or otherwise.

The Hausa men just marched up to the trestle, dropped their shorts and took their beatings without a murmur, got up and put their shorts on again, as if nothing had happened.

Others at the end of the queue were hopping about, hardly daring to look and sweating and crying in fear. As their turn came some had to be dragged to the trestle and held still by other prisoners. I dreaded these days.

I also did weekly inspections of the prison, never on a fixed day so they never knew when I would visit. I had to inspect the kitchen, food stores, back-room latrines and also the various housing blocks, and check the sleeping quarters for bedbug infestations.

In spite of all this, during the wet season the prisoners had to be doubly checked in, as often men tried to enter the prison! At least in prison there was shelter from the elements and regular good meals, which was more than what many had outside.

8.
A HANGING

My duties in the Government Prison included the witnessing of a judicial hanging. Without a doubt of all my experiences this was the worst.

A young man was accused of murder and after a protracted trial lasting many months he was found guilty and sentenced to death. Then another long wait until the prison authorities received a sealed letter from His Majesty's Government in London, allowing the death sentence to be carried out.

During all this time, Musa, the accused, was kept in isolation in the punishment block. Prisoners being punished had to work breaking stones with a small hammer. They were each given a large pile of rocks and by the end of the day they had to have broken them into chips.

Musa was housed here in a lock-up cell on his own but did not have to do any stone breaking, in fact he had nothing to do all day except watch the others, or stare at the dreary high wall and the sky.

He was handcuffed and wore shackles on both ankles. He had found a piece of grass to hold up the centre of the chain to make walking a bit easier and to prevent chafing of his ankles. I got to know him quite well as I had to see him every week, checking his weight and stools, and treating a worm infection and any other diseases. He was kept in good physical condition. I always knew when Musa was coming to the prison dispensary by the sound of the clanking of the chains and his shuffle.

Eventually the sealed letter arrived from London, no reprieve, and the date of execution was set for three weeks' time at eight o'clock in the morning. Musa was transferred to the condemned cell block right next door to the scaffold room. I had to see him daily during this time to keep him fit and to maintain his morale as much as possible.

The carpenters were brought in, the scaffold polished, the trapdoor hinges were well greased, the trap lever cleaned and oiled, and the floor below ground cleaned and brushed. The executioner was summoned and the special hangman's rope attached to the cross-beam. Musa was weighed and measured for the umpteenth time, as the 'drop' depends on the weight and height of the individual. The corset leathers and buckles were cleaned and loosened; this is a device to ensure the convicted prisoner stands up straight prior to the release of the trapdoor. It is made of thin strips of wood joined together with pieces of leather; once strapped around a man he is unable to bend down. Throughout the three weeks poor Musa could hear all these preparations next door.

The appointed day arrived and I had to meet the officials

and the senior prison officer. There we assembled: senior prison officer, chief of police, the legal attorney and myself. There was an eerie quiet: no outside work parties on this day and all the prisoners were inside.

Right on time the chief warder ushered us out into the prison where we marched in single file to the condemned cell block. The only noise was the crunching of our footsteps on the paths. It was horrifying. We marched past Musa who was crying and writhing about in fear. There was a mullah with him trying to comfort him and saying prayers. We took our positions around the trapdoor, the rope hanging down in readiness. The senor prison officer glanced around to check that everything was in order, the hangman checked the rope and the knots again. The prison officer then nodded to the hangman and the chief warder picked up what looked like a canvas bucket, the hood, and they both went down to collect Musa. They escorted him up the stairs still wearing leg irons, with his hands handcuffed behind his back.

The hangman put the noose around his neck, making sure that the knot was in the right place at the side. At the moment that the trapdoor lever was about to be pulled, Musa began to wriggle and bend his knees. He needed to stand upright, so the senior prison officer went forward with one foot on the trapdoor and with one hand pressed Musa's chest backwards, the other hand on his buttocks pulling forward to get him vertical. Then the hangman pulled the lever and Musa dropped out of sight. The loose coils of rope whipped off the cross-beam.

We had to peer over the trapdoor where we could see the body spinning around at the end of the rope, with the encased head lolling to one side.

We then all marched in file back to the senior officer's office, ashen-faced and sweating, deeply shaken by the experience, all except the prison officer who had witnessed many judicial hangings.

Silently we went our separate ways. I had to return in one hour's time, to do a post-mortem examination to be sure that it was a proper judicial hanging, i.e. that the odontoid process[5] of the second cervical vertebra had broken the spinal cord.

So for the second time I entered the prison carrying my medical bag with my instruments, apron and gear. This time the prison had come back to life and there was the usual bustle. I was hardly noticed as I went to the condemned cell block, accompanied by a couple of warders and two strapping prisoners who took Musa to the small post-mortem room adjacent to the scaffold.

I opened up the slaughtered Musa and found that he was judicially hanged and I signed the necessary forms to this effect and handed them over to the senior prison officer.

So ended the life of Musa rightly or wrongly.

This was and still is a haunting nightmare of mine.

5　The skull rests on the first vertebra of the vertebral column. This first vertebra is broad and shallow, supporting the skull. It is also known as the atlas vertebra. The second vertebra is known as the axis, and has a peg of bone (odontoid process) that projects upwards and allows the atlas vertebra to rotate around it. If the neck is rapidly hyperextended, such as in a hanging, the odontoid process snaps and death occurs due to crushing of the spinal cord.

9.
HEALTH 'SISTERING'

Once a month I accompanied the Health Sister to one of her clinics, as it was so far and so difficult to reach.

We drove about thirty miles out on a tarred road and then turned off onto a bush road of laterite, with a very bad surface. We continued for another ten miles or so through a tobacco plantation, until we came to a river.

We left the car there and carried our medical bags, until we met some young men from the village who relieved us of our gear. I forded the river, which was shallow, but Sister was carried over, piggyback fashion.

We clambered up the steep banks on the other side and went through the main street of the village. It was a fascinating place.

The street was lined with neem trees. Apparently, these trees had been imported from India many years ago and had really flourished here. There is no known disease, virus or insect which attacks them. The local people hold this exogenous tree in high regard, as every part of it can be used in cures. Bark, leaves, fruit (which are like green grapes), roots and its juices all have their uses.

Under the shade of the trees various craftsmen performed their trade, the tailors with their sewing machines humming as they treadled, wheels whirring. The leather workers were doing intricate designs on leather, and the trinket and tin men were making containers for wax lights. The ingenious necklace maker was making holes through semi-precious stones with a nail, using his feet and toes as a vice. He hammered away, before threading all the stones together.

Maribou storks on the river Niger, batik by Ruth Holmes

The open meat stalls were covered in flies, while vegetables and fruit were all piled up neatly in rows, ready for a quick sale.

By this time quite a crowd had collected behind us, but they soon petered off as we walked up the small escarpment to the whitewashed building that was the dispensary. The nurses were waiting for us and there were several patients to see.

An old man wearing baggy trousers came waddling up the

hill with difficulty. He was exhausted and short of breath. Was he perhaps a heart case? On examination it turned out the man had a large right hydrocele (a collection of fluid in the scrotum).[6] He sat on a chair in a corner with a bucket, which was too small for his 4-gallon hydrocele. I drained the hydrocele which filled one bucket and then a second. The patient fainted briefly, was revived and then walked jauntily home.

We went back through the village, but this time I carried Sister through the ford.

Driving back, the fan belt of my car went. I used shoelaces to fix it, replaced the water, and eventually reached home.

---

6   A hydrocele is an accumulation of fluids around a testicle, in this case due to the endemic parasitic disease spread by mosquitoes: filariasis. These small filarial parasites block lymphatic vessels and cause swelling and accumulation of lymph, causing hydroceles in scrotum or elephantiasis of the leg.

10.
TWO CASES OF RABIES

The very word Rabies sounds sinister and puts fear into one's heart in almost any language.

The disease has been known since the dawn of civilisation and was written about in Greek mythology. It is a disease caused by a virus conveyed to humans from a rabid animal as a result of a bite or lick on a scratch, most commonly from an infected dog. To date there has been only one or two known cures: the majority of cases are fatal.

My first case of human rabies was in a man who had been bitten by a 'pie-dog'. He was a big man, nearly six feet tall and eleven stone in weight when he was admitted to hospital as a suspected case of hydrophobia (fear of water). He had been bitten on his leg and the bites were cleansed daily and anti-rabies injections given. After a short while he began vomiting his food and began to crawl around his bed on all fours. At times he lay in bed and was quite lucid in his speech through his dry lips and tongue, although he was unable to swallow water and would make a peculiar barking sound. The flesh just vanished off his previously muscular body until he died. He knew exactly what was happening to him.

The second case was even more tragic. I was on tour visiting the dispensaries when a father brought along his pretty young daughter of thirteen years. Tears were in the man's eyes as he explained that his daughter had been bitten by a dog about three weeks ago and that she could not drink water and was going mad. The poor wee thing was dying to drink but, when she did, she vomited all over the place uncontrollably. She died a day or two later.[7]

I then received a message from the Catering Rest House that the cats milling around there were dying, some frothing at the mouth. So, in the company of the vet we caught several sick cats, killed them and sent their brain to the central laboratory for examination to see if they were suffering from rabies. A few days later a telegram arrived stating that they were heavily infected with the virus.

What an administration problem this was. The incubation period can be a matter of weeks or up to ten to twelve months. We had to check the Rest House register for all travellers and friends who had stayed there who might have come into contact with any of the cats.

Telegrams, telexes, the World Health Organization in Geneva, telephone calls and radio messages to all possible contacts, informing them of the possibility that they might

---

7 My father was deeply affected by these deaths and never felt able to have a pet
   dog or cat in the house after this.

have contracted rabies and that they should report to their nearest doctor or police station.

Our contacts covered the world and to my knowledge no one contracted 'cat rabies'.

A donkey died rather peculiarly and the vet took out the brains and sent it for analysis and it came back strongly positive for rabies, but we had no suspected cases of 'donkey rabies'.

11.
THE POLICEMAN'S WIFE

The police sergeant brought his wife along to see me as he was worried about her; she had six children and the youngest was aged sixteen. She had not had a period for at least five or six years. She was a short woman, about 5ft 2in, and weighed about twelve stone.

They both complained that she had got very fat over the past three or four years. Her breasts were flabby after breastfeeding all her six children, each for fifteen months or more at a time. According to them, apart from being fat and having this enormous tummy, there was nothing else the matter.

Examination of her abdomen revealed a large void mass that extended from her ribcage to her pelvis. It was fluctuant and there were no foetal parts or movement felt or seen. On auscultation no foetal heart sounds were heard. Several experienced midwives and the Matron examined the woman and unanimously diagnosed a large cystic tumour or ovarian cyst.

The positive signs of pregnancy were excluded, namely

the palpation of foetal parts, the palpation of foetal movement and hearing of the foetal heart. The common suggestive signs are enlargement of the breasts with secretion of milk, sickness, alteration in food likes and dislikes, increase in weight and swelling of the abdomen.

I made arrangements to do a laparotomy and explore and remove this large cystic tumour. On opening the abdominal cavity, I found a full-term pregnant uterus. Matron immediately summoned the midwife to get ready to receive the infant. The womb was opened and an infant was produced, but then to our surprise there was another one!

Twins! Both over 5lb and they both survived, were breastfed and supplemented: the sergeant was thrilled at the result of the operation.

Things can be difficult working in Africa, but also humbling.

12.

THE HYENA GAME

It was a market day and people of many different tribes had come by foot and by 'mammy wagon' to this monthly get-together. It was early morning and the marketplace was shrouded in a thin, wispy shroud of mist. Some traders were putting up their stalls, others just sat on the ground and spread their goods in front of them. The dust rose steadily as more and more people padded their way into the market.

The women did most of the carrying, loads perched on top of their heads, with their babies strapped onto their backs. Some pagan women, ebony-black and glistening with sweat as they walked straight-backed with heavy calabash gourds on top of their heads. Married women had a bunch of grass fore and aft, whilst the unmarried daughters and bare-breasted single girls only had the bunch of grass hanging at the back. The bunches of grass swished as they walked briskly in single file.

Dancing on market day

As the morning wore on, friends and relations greeted one another, trading started slowly, with food – maize, corn yams, nuts, cakes, sweets – bright trinkets such as bracelets, beads and gaudy bowls of every conceivable size, all made in Birmingham!

The marketplace filled up and by midday everybody was talking about the stranger walking about in their midst. He was a short, stockily built man, about 4' 10": his skin colour and facial bones did not look local. His skin was more a dark cocoa colour, his face was more rounded with massive temporal muscles which rippled as he chewed his cola nut. His head was clean-shaven, his chest was bare except for a few straggly hairs. He wore a couple of goatskins around his waist, with a piece drawn in between his legs. His limbs rippled with muscles, which seemed somehow exaggerated by his short stature. His presence took the populace of the market by surprise as this was clearly a foreigner. What made his appearance more dramatic was that he had a heavy chain at the end of which was a muzzled hyena, which he paraded around like a dog. The beast invited a common revulsion, as local people believe the hyena to be a scavenger, eating off dead bodies and snatching young babies from people's houses. It was also fabled to be a hermaphrodite. All these things are untrue of this creature, but one thing is true: it has the strongest bite of any animal.

Gradually the youngsters gathered around the stranger and his pet, and soon nearly everyone in the market drew near, but scared to get too close. Then the talking drum began its repetitive beat and soon the air was filled with expectation, the kids began hopping in time to the drumming rhythm. It was warm and sweaty in the crowd and the stranger paraded around in a circle with his hyena and when he approached the perimeter too closely, the girls shrieked and ran back.

The throbbing of the drums changed and the stranger, his body glistening, sat in the middle of the circle and began to play with the hyena as a child would play with a puppy. The hyena looked attentive. It had the typical high shoulders, long, sloping back, and miserably short tail. The hair behind its neck stood on end and the widely separated eyes stared out above his short, massive nose, which was covered in a heavy muzzle.

The crowd 'oohed' and 'aaahed', but their attitude was that anyone could do that with an animal that was chained and heavily muzzled. Once more the stranger led the hyena around. The heat was oppressive and the man's body was lathered in sweat and the goatskins he was wearing were turning black. The drumming started up again and he quickly took off the muzzle. The crowd screamed as he approached and fell back if he came too near. He returned to the centre of the ring and played and wrestled with the animal, rolling it over in the sand before putting his hand into the hyena's mouth. He let the hyena nip his ears and finally put his throat within its jaws. The crowd watched in awe, but they still thought it must be a trick and that the stranger had pulled out or filed down the creature's teeth.

The tempo of the drums quickened and changed and a few people began to leave the circle but for most curiosity prevailed, as they watched the final act by the stranger and his hyena. A well-known local butcher appeared with the thigh bone of a cow and threw it into the circle. The gleaming wee man went into a sort of dancing shuffle, collected the bone and brandished it above his head while he danced in a circle with the hyena following behind. They then returned to the sand where the stranger sat down with the thigh bone resting on his knees. On command, the hyena came towards him and neatly bit through the bone, which fell on the ground in three pieces! A terrific cheer went up from the crowd and the stranger muzzled his hyena and left.

13.
JUJU TALES

Snake Juju

This is a true story, I'm terrified of snakes and don't like them unless they are dead. When my family was coming out to see me in my bungalow, I decided that our compound should be cleared of snakes. I called the local snake man to come up and rid the garden of snakes, so it would be safe.

The afternoon came and the snake man came along and he looked in my soakage pit and septic tank and all around the house and collected a few small snakes. This was a bad time for the Egyptian viper, which is a very dangerous snake. At the end of his inspection and looking around the compound he took out a small bag from his pocket which contained a powder, this dry, brown, straw-like stuff.

He sprinkled this powder the whole way around the perimeter of the compound, the way you would sprinkle salt over your food. He said, 'You don't think my medicine will work,' whereupon he pulled out the bag in which he had the other snakes and threw three or four snakes back into the compound.

The snakes slithered along to where he had sprinkled the brown powder and sure enough they buckled, as though there was an invisible wire netting. They went right along the edge where he had sprinkled, which I had marked between two plants, and the snakes would not go across this line. Finally he went around and picked up all the snakes and I never saw another snake in my compound ever again.

I also heard of a police officer who was petrified of snakes so he went to the local Juju man, who promised that he could give him a treatment so that snakes would not see him. He pondered over this a long time as he was so frightened of them and decided to get the treatment.

The Juju man then made various incantations and did several scarifications, a bit like a smallpox inoculation. He did one on the outside of the man's leg, one on an arm and another over his shoulder blade. He smeared some 'medicine' into the small cuts and told the man to come back in a week's time. The police officer did so and a few more incantations took place. Then the Juju man said to him, 'No snake will see you now, so let's try and see it working.' Together they walked out into the bush, followed by a throng of young village boys. It was not long before they found a puff-adder, all coiled up with its head resting on its coils ready to strike. The officer was terrified but the Juju man told him to walk up to the snake. He was shaking like a leaf and the sweat was pouring off him, but as he approached the adder rolled over to allow its white belly to the sun. He walked backwards and the snake reorientated itself, but as soon as he approached it again it turned over.

Thief Juju

There are many things in this life that we can't understand and when fully understood could well be a great advance in medicine, if we could only find the secrets.

A married couple who lived in a two-storey, well-built house were sleeping in a double bed enveloped in a large mosquito net, which was tucked around under the mattress. They kept a Dachshund which was a particularly good house dog: no one could ever approach the house without it yapping.

The lady got up in the morning to go to the kitchen to make some tea and she noticed that her dog had made a mess over the drawing room carpet: she thought that this was strange as they had taken it for its usual nightly walk, and their dog would never do anything like that.

She made the tea and brought the tray upstairs to her husband and began untucking the mosquito net, when she noticed a big hole in it at the end of the bed. She then looked for her handbag which she kept under the pillow, between her and her husband: it was gone.

How did the 'thief men' get into the house without disturbing the yappy dog, climb up the stairs, then walk right into the bedroom where two people were sleeping, without the aid of drugs or alcohol, cut through the net which was about three or four inches away from their ears, all without waking them? Possibly an anaesthetic powder that could be puffed into the room?

A senior police officer did not believe in this Juju and scoffed at the idea, so he made an arrangement with the suspected thief men to try robbing him on a particular night, the deal being that he would get back anything that they stole from him. He kept an enormous Labrador, a marvellous guard dog who would keep anyone at bay until he called the dog away. He went to bed quite happily, knowing that an attempt was going to be made to rob him that night, but felt quite secure with his faithful Labrador.

The following morning he woke up at first light feeling a bit cold and no wonder: he was lying only on a sheet, the blankets, even the underblanket, were off his bed, the sheets were there – but no blankets. The mosquito net was still tucked around his bed and there was not a stick of furniture left in his bedroom. His Labrador came up to him as usual, wagging his tail and gave him a friendly lick.

Juju medicine

There is also medicine to prevent hyenas from seeing you and another for lions: how these work no one has yet discovered ...

Poisoning one's enemies used to be quite common. Many men keep a long little fingernail. Poison would be carried in the clothes and could be scooped up by a little fingernail and put in the food or drink whilst the victim's attention was distracted. A common poison was made from a mushroom-like fungus that caused liver failure: the person would die jaundiced, as if they had yellow fever.

There was a scruffy little village near a lake that was the Harley Street of tribal medicine. People with all kinds of different diseases used to go to get 'cured', even coming from other countries. It was alleged that every year a virgin was given to the lake crocodiles to placate them. This also enhanced the powers of the village elders in curing ills.

I once had a patient in hospital who was dying of an inoperable cancer in her abdomen. It was an enormous hard, solid mass and the woman was just skin and bone. The husband asked me if I would mind if he brought in the Juju man to see if he could help his wife; I had no hesitation in allowing him to try, as her case was utterly hopeless.

The Juju man came in one evening when I was not there and gave the woman a bowl of water into which he had sprinkled some powdery material. She gamely swallowed this adulterated water and she immediately began to gag and retch. She brought up several small, hard, gristle-like pellets which pinged into the now empty bowl, and the Juju man said she was now cured.

From then on she put on weight, the masses in her abdomen disappeared and she never looked back. I could hardly believe it, but she was 'cured' and was discharged from hospital after about two weeks, when she had regained her strength.

14.

THREE WIVES AND A MURDER

A Murder

Sirens wailed and blue lights flashed as the police Land Rover came careering up to the hospital while I was seeing about 300 patients. A breathless inspector rushed in to collect me: a clerk had just murdered his wife and they wanted me to see the body before anything was disturbed.

It was 8.15 am on a cool, bright, sunny morning when the inspector brought me to the field where the dead woman was lying, face downwards, with bloodstained froth around her mouth and nostrils, and inky-black bloodstains on the recently tilled earth. The buzz of flies filled the air and her back was black with bluebottles.

The police photographer took all the necessary shots of the body before I turned her over. The front of her blouse was torn and bloodstained. There were some deep cuts across her palms where she had tried to protect herself, as well as cuts about her neck. I would need to examine her later in the mortuary to assess the degree of her injuries. The police took some more photographs and the body was transferred to the hospital mortuary.

The inspector then told me the story. The clerk and his wife had a row first thing in the morning and she had threatened him with a carving knife. He got angry and snatched the knife from her. She hit him in the 'privates', which sent him wild, so he stabbed her several times and ran out of the house. She gave chase for about fifty yards then collapsed from the loss of blood. The clerk walked to the police station holding the carving knife, with his shirt splattered in blood, and said, "I've just killed my wife." It was then that the police went to the scene of the crime and the inspector came to find me.

We went back to the house where the couple lived and could confirm the clerk's statement by the bloodstains on the floor and the furniture in disarray. We stepped outside and followed the trail made by the spurts of blood from the dying woman.

When I examined her in the mortuary, amongst her many wounds I found a small puncture of one of the main arteries in the base of the neck. This was what had finally killed her.

Later that day the clerk was brought up to the hospital, where I treated the cuts on his hands. The last time I saw him he was in prison garb, wearing handcuffs and leg irons in the condemned cell block.

A Case of Attempted Murder

In this case, the husband was fed up with his wife and he belted her one across the head. When she was unconscious he decided that the best place to get rid of her was to throw her down the well in his compound.

She survived this terrible ordeal and, hearing her yells, the neighbours became suspicious and called the police.

The police fished her out of the well and, when the husband saw her being brought up still alive, he decided to kill himself. He tried to cut his throat with a razor, but it was a poor attempt. The police rushed him to the hospital and I sewed up the superficial gashes that he had made on his throat.

He was admitted and kept under guard during his time on the wards. His wife was brought in, too, and admitted to the female ward for observation to check that she had no skull fractures or other injuries. She seemed none the worse for her ordeal down the well. After a few days, however, she began to act peculiarly: from being quite cooperative and helpful she withdrew and became uncommunicative. Her husband was discharged from the hospital and the police took him to the local prison pending his trial.

The wife became more and more withdrawn, refusing food and nursing care, soiling her bed and lying curled up in a foetal position. She stubbornly refused any attempts to help her, even pulling out intravenous drips.

We could not do any more for her in the hospital so we had to send her to the female mental wing of the prison. This shocking place was supervised by excellent female warders. Their charges ranged from the seriously mentally disturbed and psychotic, some of whom were caged up, to prostitutes with no mental illness, nursing their babies. The sane inmates prepared the food provided by the prison authority and helped the wardresses to look after those who were mentally ill.

Food was left in the wife's cell, but she would never take it if watched. By now she had become completely uncommunicative and she lived and played with her excreta when no one was looking. She was in a semi-coma and completely unresponsive even on painful stimuli; she had no blink reflex and she just lay curled up on her mat even if she was carried outside into the sun. There was absolutely no recognition of sound, or response to light or pain.

She remained in this state for two and a half years, becoming just skin and bone, a living corpse. Her husband was in the same prison and came to see her several times but could do absolutely nothing for her. Indeed he was distressed to see her in such a pitiful state.

By this time a new asylum had been built, about 250 miles away, and a visiting psychiatrist suggested that she should spend her remaining days there. So arrangements were made with the asylum and the prison wardress was to accompany this poor woman by road.

She was carried into the back of the Land Rover with a mat over the mattress, and two wardresses sitting on either side of her, and off they went on the long, bumpy journey.

To the utter astonishment of the wardresses they then heard a voice speaking and it was the patient! They were dumbfounded when she asked for her possessions – bracelet, necklace, purse etc – which the police had taken from her three years ago!

By the time they reached the asylum, she was sitting up and talking quite rationally. The asylum supervisor was utterly amazed to see her in this condition after all the medical reports that he had on her and the preparations made for her reception at the hospital.

She remained in the asylum for a mere three weeks, and was then discharged home. Her husband remained in prison, pending his trial for attempted murder.

A Case of Wife Beating

My telephone rings at one-twenty in the middle of the night and the nurse on duty speaks down the phone rather agitatedly:

"Doctor! A man has brought along his wife who he has beaten up! I have informed the theatre staff and they will be ready soon, please come quickly as she is bleeding quite a bit."

"Why, Nurse, what did he beat her with?"

"He beat her with a sword, Doctor."

"My God. I'll be down right away."

The woman was lying in the anteroom to the theatre on a trolley and was just about conscious. Her face was completely splattered in blood which had congealed. Her ragged clothes were in ribbons, all thick with clotted blood. Beside her, squatting on the floor, was an elderly man looking very sorry for himself, with a few bloodstains on his <u>riga</u>.[8] He was the husband.

---

8 Robe.

I set up a drip of dextrose saline as we had no blood, and started to examine her injuries. Her scalp was cleft in two from forehead to the back of her skull and her hair was all matted and stuck together with congealed blood. There were several small gashes on her cheeks. A massive slice had been made into her right shoulder muscle mass. On both forearms there were a number of deep cuts on the inner side, where she had tried to protect herself by raising her arms. We took her into the theatre and gave her an anaesthetic, so that we could have a better look and sew her up, after giving her a good clean-up and appropriate anti-tetanus injections.

We clamped bleeding points and started to clean and tidy up the larger wounds. The one in her scalp took a long time, as the sword had scraped along the vault of her skull, leaving a shallow trough. The gaping wound in her shoulder had to be repaired in layers as it was so deep: first, the muscles were opposed and joined up, then the tissues under the skin and then finally the skin. Some of the numerous cuts in her arms took quite a time to repair and explore to remove any dead tissue or pieces of clothing material; the smaller cuts were very superficial and only needed to be cleaned and dressed.

When we had just about finished I had a look at the small lacerations about her face. To my horror the lower jaw was completely shattered, it felt like marbles in a cloth bag. Her gums and teeth were uneven, but were not loose in the mouth.

We then attempted to wire the teeth together to get some stability to the jaw. I decided to send her to another hospital for specialist surgical attention. We fixed her as best we could and made her comfortable. It was seven o'clock by the time we got her to the ward.

I now spent a frantic time arranging for a plane to take her about 300 miles to see the Dental Surgeon and Orthopaedic Specialist. I was lucky this time, as there was a small mission plane in the district and the pilot agreed to take her.

What a business this turned out to be, a stretcher case going into the tiny cockpit of this small, single-engine aircraft. We squeezed her in, plus husband, the pilot said a prayer and off they flew into the skies. I then had to arrange for an ambulance to meet the aircraft at the other end and arrange admission through the consultant surgeon.

Eventually I heard that she was discharged with a functioning jaw and that the government police were investigating the 'assault'.

15.
THE BLADDER STONE

I was based for a while in Sokoto in Northern Nigeria and I would go into the bush by camel. On one of these tours I stayed in a small village in a hut which had been swept and tidied and where my servant put up my camp bed with its mosquito net, along with a table and a chair.

My nurse had already seen the village head and arranged that we hold an evening clinic under the tree in the centre of the village. The village head got his drummer to beat out on his 'talking drum' the message that the doctor was here and that anyone who had ulcers, sore eyes or any other sickness should come just before sundown to the village tree, where they would be seen and get medicine.

A few stragglers turned up and we dressed ulcers with a clean antiseptic dressing, cleaner than the standard dressing of dried cow dung and leaves. As well as the usual variety of venereal diseases, there were several untreated cases of leprosy, where we advised how to get urgent treatment and informed the village head of the actions needed to stop this devastating disease.[9]

Seeing patients on tour

I was then asked to examine a young boy of about ten. He was lying on the sand in agony, with a constant desire to void urine but, except for tiny drops, he was unable to do so. He was in severe pain and had sores around his groin from the constant dampness, with the added annoyance of the myriads of flies buzzing around

9 There were widespread mistaken beliefs about leprosy that generated fear and stigmatisation. However, leprosy was a curable disease at this time, because since the early 1950s an effective oral treatment (dapsone) had been introduced. Leprosy was curable if treated early, but left untreated it could lead to terrible, crippling deformities, dis[Figurement, blindness and isolation.

him: he was truly a pathetic sight.

On examining his abdomen, I could feel an enormous hard mass in the lower part of his tummy. A large bladder stone was obviously the cause of the young boy's suffering. As time and dates were unknown in the bush, we worked out the times of the moon and told the boy's mother to bring him into the hospital in Sokoto on the next moon's first quarter.

The new quarter came and, sure enough, the boy arrived at the hospital sitting on a camel, led by his mother.

The hospital staff were already on the lookout for them and I was delighted to see them. They both seemed to be pleased to see me again. But the boy was terrified, as this was the first time he had been out of his village, and he was now a three-night camel march away from home.

He had never seen men walking around in white coats and the hospital ward also alarmed him: beds, electric lights, fans and other equipment he had never seen before. We gave him some time to adjust to these surroundings before operating on him.

Operating proved to be difficult as the stone was wedged into the internal meatus of the urethra and I had to use some force and manipulation to remove it. Anyway, the operation was completed and he returned to the ward.

The first few post-operative days were a bit stormy, but the boy gradually got better and the wound healed up well. He was pleased he had no more pain and, at last, he could now pass urine normally. However, his fear of this strange environment was a major concern and it was a great relief when eventually the camel arrived to take him home. Amidst cheers from the theatre and ward staff the boy set off riding the camel, escorted by his mother, on the long journey back to his village in the bush.

16.
JOEY PIE

Joey Pie was special: a mixture of a Labrador and a pie-dog, known far and wide around Sokoto. He was a sturdy dog with a grizzled look and grey hairs between his eyes. He had battle scars from his youth and all dogs respected his kingship and superiority. Everyone agreed that he was a highly intelligent dog, who behaved beautifully.

Joey Pie never missed a party. The times of day, venue or host, might change but he was always there. He arrived before the first guest, so it was not because he had seen cars drawing up. There were many theories as to how he knew. Were there special tasks undertaken by cooks or steward, such as furniture being moved, or perhaps a large dinner set or side dishes brought out, which were not always in use? Was there a lot of polishing of silver and glasses which was a signal to the dog? Uniforms being specially laundered and out on the line might have given him a clue, or, who knows, perhaps a Kingsway Store delivery, with a larger than usual order could have been a sign for Joey Pie that helped him amazingly and accurately identify just where and when the party was to be.

Joey Pie's owner was Frank Frazer who worked with the United African Company (UAC), a popular member of the Sokoto Club. Time after time Joey Pie broke one of the most important of the club rules which was 'No Dogs Allowed' and came in smiling and wagging his tail. Frank was sent a warning letter and then another. He described how he had tied the dog up and locked him in the house, certain he had been able to restrain him this time. This was a serious issue. There had been complaints about dogs in general, but not one single complaint about Joey Pie, other than he had come through the doors. It looked as if Frank would have to stay at home in the evening, if he was unable to come to the Club without being followed by his dog.

A special meeting was called to resolve the situation. Frank was living on his own at the time without his wife and family, relying on the Club for most of his social life, and he was very well liked. After a long discussion a solution was found: Joey Pie was voted a member of the Sokoto Club in his own right! There was great relief all round and everyone drank to the health of the dog and his owner.

17.
THE 'NO CHILDREN' TRIBE

This is a story of tax and education evasion. It began when the District Head had not been getting enough revenue and the children from certain areas were not attending school.

Concern was raised that this particular hill tribe might be dying from some mysterious disease and so I was requested to come in to see the District Head for a briefing and then recruit reliable porters to go with me to find out what had happened.

I headed out towards a village I was told was 'just up a hill' and then drove six to eight miles over rough tracks looking for it. I stopped in a small village at the bottom of a long, U-shaped valley, which was lightly wooded on the lower slopes above a meandering stream.

Shaba my houseboy unloaded all my kit from the car: 'chop box', bedding, blankets, mosquito net, bath, basin, two medicine chests, a bush chair, Tilley lamps and kerosene. I carried my 12-bore double shotgun, hoping to bag some guinea fowl or bush fowl for supper.

The porters said that the village was "just up that mountain" and pointed to a faint outline I could barely see in the blue sky ahead, so off we went in single file up the valley. There was no breeze at all and it was oppressively hot. The chatter of the black and white monkeys was constant, and we now and again we glimpsed their faces with bushy beards. Parakeets were whirring through the trees and, as we went further into the valley, it became even hotter. We had marched about eight miles and now the trees had been cleared and we passed through agricultural land with guinea corn, sweet potatoes and yams growing.

Bearers on tour

We had reached the apex of the valley, with a slope almost 90 degrees on either side, when the head porter exclaimed that there was the village up there. There were countless brown paths between the boulders and people were going up and down as if on a street. I looked up vertically in horror. I saw the ramparts of the village above me, but I just did not know how I could make it. Contemplating the situation, I asked one of the porters to get me a strong stick. They were laughing happily while they transported all my kit up this terrible incline, so, taking a deep breath and armed with my stick and 12-bore I started the ascent. After ten minutes we were all puffing and blowing and I had to hand over my 12-bore to Shaba. We would take one or two steps then halt and breathe deeply then one, two, three or maybe four steps upwards over the slippery paths, strewn with rocks and stones. Eventually the porters put down their loads and had a halfway halt. I reached them ten minutes later, puffing and blowing and cursing myself for all the cigarettes I had smoked and beer I had drunk, because of which I now found myself so out of training. My lungs were bursting and I feared for my life, balancing as I was with a sheer drop below me. The porters continually warned me not to dislodge any stones for I could start an avalanche or even kill someone.

I was amazed to watch the men and women go up and down the mountain like goats. They weren't even out of breath and I was told that they often made the trip two or three times a day.

My throat was parched and all I wanted was a cool drink. I dared not look down the valley or I felt sick. When I did finally reach the crest, the porters were all there to welcome me and the loads had been deposited at the house the village head had allocated to me. Never were warm beer and pots and pots of tea, produced by Shaba, so welcome.

I dreaded how I was to get down again, perhaps sliding on my bottom?

A little later I made the acquaintance of the new District Head, only recently installed, following the death of the previous head three months before.

It was strange not to see or hear babies and toddlers. Usually when we arrived in a village they ran around looking at me in amazement as something out of their world. Here were young men and young women of both sexes but no children. Some old women seemed to have what looked like groundnuts on their heads; on closer inspection I realised they were made of mud. The hairdresser gets a twirl of hair and incorporates it into a pellet of mud. The final result looks really elegant – a reddish berried hairdo!

Shaba had in the meantime put up my bed and washbasin, lit the Tilley lamp and started getting my supper ready. He had made a number of friends as everyone was very interested in the peculiar objects he had and how he was using them. This was the first time many had seen a European and I was certainly the first doctor they had ever met.

I was utterly exhausted that first night and went to bed early. I lay under my mosquito net listening to the quiet chatter of Shaba and his new friends, telling them, I am sure, all sorts of stories of the civilised world.

It was a clear and starry night and I lay half in and half out of my hut. A pie-dog barked, the cockerel crowed, and the fruit bats shrieked and zoomed around the trees. I could not, I know, have heard the high-pitched sounds of the cicadas so high up, but I would have heard baby cries and there were none.

I felt as safe as houses in my camp bed, with the mosquito net tucked in. I lay thinking of the trip I had made up the mountain and again wondered how on earth I would make it down again. Eventually I dropped off to sleep. Suddenly I awoke to a cacophony of sound. There was screaming and tin cans were being battered to a most irregular beat. The sound emanated from nearby and increased, as young men shouted as they danced around the village. Occasionally there was a shriek of a female. The noise continued on and off throughout the whole night, becoming more intense as they passed my house. It would stop suddenly and just as I was about to drop off to sleep it would start again. It finally ceased about an hour before dawn and I felt exhausted as Shaba made my bacon and eggs.

Characteristic tribal hair adornment of red mud

I had arranged with the village head that I would see anyone who was sick, in the centre of the village under the tree. So after breakfast Shaba took my chair, table and medical chest to the appointed tree. I took my camera, sat down and waited to see what would happen.

It was an extraordinary experience sitting there with perhaps a hundred people, who peeped at me to see if I was real or not. I noticed that many of these people had enlarged thyroid glands. Some of these were really enormous and I could hear them breathe through their narrowed windpipes, like a broken horse.

On that first morning, I did not see many patients. However, I did find out what all the noise the previous night was about. It was the three-month anniversary of the death of the late District Head. This was a pagan tribe so they did not believe in the Prophet Mohamed and unlike Shaba, did not pray four times a day.

The terrible noise was to represent the old District Head's prowess. He had made many women fertile and had many wives and many children and his 'ghost' – a carved phallic wooden ornament – was taken round the whole village. The drumming and the tins were beaten to warn the virgins and women to stay out of sight, for if any female should see the wooden symbol she would then be barren. She would no longer have sexual allure or be attractive to any man.

I noticed that the men wore a simple sort of headgear and a loincloth and nothing else, but all of them seemed to have a hole in what I thought of as their 'sporrans', with a cornstalk talisman protruding forwards. In fact, this was a beautifully fashioned sheath made from grass and plaited like a 'Chinese Finger', which they put onto their member. While hoeing with their legs apart, the penis was vulnerable, particularly to snake bite. It was also in view of the women, who were hoeing behind, and so they had woven this protection.

Goitres (commonly seen due to lack of iodine)

In an attempt to bring in the families I thought it would be a good idea to ask the village head to arrange a dance for me in the evening. He did so and there were two or three drummers and old grannies with their red, nutty hairdos. Quite a few of them had been to the hairdresser's. These dignified old ladies formed themselves into a line and shuffled forward towards me, their feet thumping in time to the drumming. They wore heavy anklets made of bronze, and on top of their feet were tied old rags to protect them from the constant banging of the two or three heavy bracelets. As they all got into the rhythmic stamping, they thumped towards me, bracelets clashing, then, when a few feet away they would turn round and go back again. Imperceptibly the drumming tempo increased, as did the thumping and clashing, producing dust that covered the whole area, so that the feet of the dancers could no longer be seen. Only their sweaty heads and sopping wet upper bodies were visible.

The dancers moving to and fro, to and fro, lasted a long time and at the end they were exhausted. A crowd had gathered out of curiosity and it was then that at last I heard a baby's whimper. The dance progressed and this time the younger generation teenagers did the same to and fro shuffle.

It was a marvellous experience to see this spectacle under the stars, with stage lighting provided very effectively by my Tilley lamp hanging on the branch of the neem tree.

I called a halt in order to get some sleep and because I felt that those who had been working in the fields would feel the same, but no, for that night the young men joined in. However, during the occasional quiet period I again heard babies' cries.

On my second morning there appeared to be a happier air about the place, with everyone laughing and talking about the dance. I saw several dancers with the top half of their feet raw from the heavy bracelets, which I duly treated.

When evening arrived and the drummers started up again, the villagers collected under the baobab tree and impromptu dancing began in little groups at first. Then, as more and more people began to collect, lo and behold, a little youngster, absolutely naked, came running up one of the lanes and started to shuffle. That started it! Dozens of children appeared from nowhere. It was still daylight and there was a brightness and happiness now in the groups, as mothers began to bring their babies to me with sicknesses that had been worrying them. By and large they were a very healthy tribe, except for the result of their lack of iodine, which gave them this endemic goitre.

That night was a quieter one and only a couple of times did I hear some rushing around, with screaming and the beating of tins.

On the third morning, as I was busy examining a host of children who had now magically appeared, the village head came over to see me and to say how pleased he was that I was staying in his hut and honouring him. He said he was looking forward to me coming and promised that there would be dancing. He then asked that I would bring my Tilley lamp along with me as it was the only one in the place!

18.

His Head Was Not Correct[10]

In early July 1959 in Ilorin the police were informed that a body had been buried on the outskirts of the town. The police took my colleague to the site where the remains of a corpse were exhumed in 'piecemeal' fashion. I was assigned to do the post-mortem examination and without exaggeration it took me over twenty minutes to enter the mortuary, as the smell was so terrible.

All the soft tissues were liquefied, only the bones and the ligaments remained. Practically all the essential bones were accounted for, but the hyoid bone,[11] was amongst those missing, even after a careful search through the debris and maggots.

A day or two later, after several showers of rain, I inspected the burial site in company with the police. After poking about we

---

10 This article appeared in the Medical Services Newsletter, October 1961
11 During a post-mortem the hyoid bone is key in determining death by strangulation

found several carpal and metacarpal bones, as well as the hyoid bone which was intact. All these small bones had been brought to the surface by the rain.

During this time the Nigerian Police were conducting intensive investigations to find out more about this body, which had not been buried according to Muslim rites, but in a very shallow grave between bushes and which had only recently been dug. To be in such a state of putrefaction the body must have been at least six weeks old, whilst the grave was only a matter of days old. It appeared that the culprits had found that the body of their victim was getting a bit high where they had hidden him and decided to move him to a more airy place.

Anyway, the police were hot on the trail and had eight lads who were under suspicion.

At 6.15 pm on Sunday 19th July I had just completed my evening round when the compound nurse informed me that the police had brought in another corpse at around 3 pm, a man who had committed suicide and had died from cut-throat injuries. It was dusk, and as the next day was a Monday when business is brisk in the hospital, I decided to do the post-mortem examination there and then.

The compound nurse went for the various papers authorising me to do the examination, collected a couple of labourers and off we went to the mortuary. The odour of the previous corpse still was very high and it took me ten minutes or so to get used to it and enter the room. I had given up smoking six months before and perhaps my olfactory nerve endings were a little more sensitive.

On the slab, all rolled up in a mat and tied up with native rope, was the body. At the foot end of the bundle was a bunch of leaves. The labourers broke the ropes and unrolled the mat. The man was wearing the long 'under riga' which was drenched in blood. As I went over to peer at an enormous gash wound in his neck, to my horror the 'corpse' grunted. He was still alive! My staff went pale with fright and I started back on the cigarettes again!

He was immediately taken to the theatre and given the works, Coramine, oxygen, Dextro, saline drip etc. I rang and asked my colleague and boss, Dr Zammit, to come immediately, and to inform the police. When the police arrived, they recognised the man as one of the band who were under suspicion for murder of the previous man who had been in the mortuary. Numerous photographs were taken and with the aid of Tilley lamps the wound was explored under a light general anaesthesia with no intubation. My notes read:

"Deep suprahyoid laceration of the neck extending from the angles of the jaw, each lateral corner of the wound serrated. Large mid-flap of skin present from superior end. No tentative cuts present. Tongue cleanly cut right to its base. No vital structures severed, but the wound extends just deep to the mucous membrane of the oropharynx which bulged out into the base of the wound on breathing. Wound closed in layers. No drain."

Was this suicide or attempted murder? The wound looked as if a sharp instrument had been used and pushed into the neck under the angle of the jaw to the other side and sawed forwards, creating this undercut superior flap.

Post-operatively the patient did extraordinarily well, considering. He was in the side ward under constant watch by at least one or two policemen. Stitches were removed on the eighth post-operative day, healing by first intention. On the tenth post-operative day, he stuck his fingers into the scar and tried to rip himself open again. Neither the hospital staff nor the policeman who were on 'constant' watch knew anything about it.

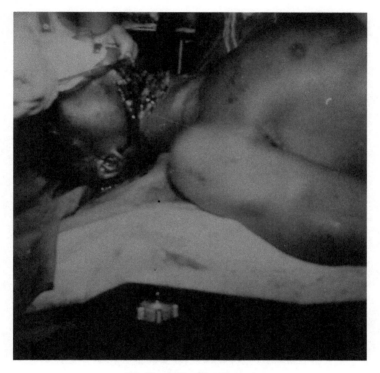

His Head Was Not Correct

Apparently before the patient had attempted to commit suicide he felt that his head "was not correct" so the obvious thing to do was to get rid of it. He tried this with an ordinary local cut-throat razor. With the thumb, index and middle finger of the left hand he pinched up a fold of skin in the midline of his neck, about the Adam's apple area, then, holding the razor in his right hand, sawed through from front to back.

The skull still adorns my office; I am not allowed to keep it in the house. Since writing this I am thinking of giving up the cigs again.

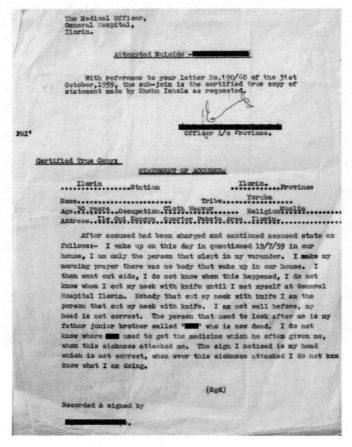

The Medical Officer,
General Hospital,
Ilorin.

Attempted Suicide – ██████████

With reference to your letter No.190/60 of the 31st October,1959, the sub-join is the certified true copy of statement made by Shehu Ishola as requested.

PBI'   Officer i/c Province.

Certified True Copy:

STATEMENT OF ACCUSED.

Ilorin ....Station   Ilorin...........Province

Name................................ Tribe.......Yoruba..........
Age..30.Years...Occupation.Cloth.Weaver...... Religion.Muslim.........
Address..Ile.Oni.Kangun..Quarter.Pakata.Area..Ilorin...............

After accused had been charged and cautioned accused state as follows:- I wake up on this day in questioned 19/7/59 in our house, I am only the person that slept in my varander. I make my morning prayer there was no body that wake up in our house. I then went out side, I do not know when this happened, I do not know when I cut my neck with knife until I met myself at General Hospital Ilorin. Nobody that cut my neck with knife I am the person that cut my neck with knife. I am not well before, my head is not correct. The person that used to look after me is my father junior brother called "███" who is now dead. I do not know where ███ used to get the medicine which he often given me, when this sickness attacked me. The sign I noticed is my head which is not correct, when ever this sickness attacked I do not know what I am doing.

(Sgd)

Recorded & signed by

██████████.

My head is not correct' statement of attempted suicide. Sadly, it also states how this individual with psychosis used to be cared for by an uncle who gave him his medication, but the brother had died.

19.

THE SULTAN'S STORY

I arrived at the Rest House in Sokoto tired and weary after motoring the 300 miles from Kaduna. My wife and I were shown to our chalet by the friendly steward. We unpacked superficially, had a wash and the steward brought us a refreshing cup of tea, the usual thick Delft cups with the green ring around the top.

Following this we took a run in the car to see what the Government Reserved Area (GRA) was like. Just before we passed the Residency, an enormous snake wriggled across the road, I wonder whether this was an omen or Juju for what was to follow…

We had returned to the Rest House to change when there was a knock on the door. There appeared a large, foreign-looking man with a shaved pate. Some of his teeth had large gold inlays and he spoke with a guttural accent, which turned out to be Polish. This was the doctor who I was relieving, and he introduced himself, his wife and his enormous Alsatian dog.

Next day the Polish doctor took me around the hospital and

introduced me to the staff. We were then taken by his driver to meet the Resident in charge of the whole province and whose superior was the Governor of the region. The Resident welcomed me to his province and thanked the Polish doctor for all he had done, wishing him a happy leave. Speaking in fluent Hausa, the Resident called to his messenger to get his driver, and he presented us with the Union Jack pennant, flying from the radiator of his car. The Polish doctor and I followed behind and off we went to be introduced to the Sultan at his palace.

We passed the hospital and went on into the town, which was built of mud; there were donkeys wandering about and goats eating rubbish. In the grounds of the Native Authority Offices stood a tree festooned with pelicans. The tree was practically white from their droppings; these migratory birds came here every year to nest and bring up their chicks.

We approached a square in the centre of town, on the right side of which was a high wall of hard mud. Within the wall was a high, fort-like structure over the main gateway. Here were several Native Authority policemen each wearing a red fez, blue drill shirt and shorts with a thick, red cummerbund around the middle with a Sam Browne on top of it; then putteed legs, some with boots and others barefoot.

The Resident's car went right through the gateway and we followed. One of the policemen opened the door for us and we got out, adjusting our ties and putting on our jackets.

The Sultan's Chief Scribe came to meet the Resident who in turn introduced me. The Scribe was a small man with a thin and sparsely grown strip of beard. He wore a red fez surrounded by a loosely folded turban, and long, white flowing robes which he kept hitching up onto his shoulders. On his feet he was wearing leather slippers decorated in colourful designs. He carried a pink file in his hand and a pen and pencil.

After bowing and shaking our fists at one another (the Hausa greeting to show that you were not armed) we shook hands and then he ushered the Resident, Polish doctor and me to the Sultan's palace. We walked through the courtyard where there were horses tethered to mushroom-shaped pegs in the hard ground; in front of us was this large, whitewashed domed building with narrow slits of windows.

Sitting and standing in front of the door were the Sultan's bodyguards, fantastically attired in their voluminous red, blue and yellow gowns and colourful turbans. Each one of his bodyguards was a specialist in his own trade or profession. The keeper of horses was an expert in everything to do with keeping them and treating them if they were sick. There was the snake man who caught and handled very poisonous snakes and knew a good deal about animal Juju medicine that would make a snake roll onto its back on your approach when you were wearing the right sort of talisman or Juju. Then there was the jester who could relieve tensions by making people laugh and doing fantastic tricks like holding a red-hot bowl in his palms without burning himself.

We weaved our way through this colourful band, waving fists, to see the Sultan at the door of his meeting chamber. His head was supported by outsized white tulle going along under his nose. He shook his fist at us in greeting and then pulled down the tulle to his chin as he greeted us.

Crowds waiting to greet the Sultan

The greeting procedure took quite some minutes as he welcomed us each of us in turn, in Hausa. It was a simple and moving experience with no hurry, as he enquired about our health: were we happy and well, were our families happy and well? He then introduced us to all his counsellors and we shook hands with them all and shook our clenched fists; some spoke to us in perfect English and others in Hausa.

The Sultan then sat on his throne, a huge chair covered in carpets and colourful pillows. He spoke slowly in Hausa to the Resident and to us so that we could pick up what he said. He pointed out chairs which had appeared for us to sit on, while his counsellors sat around on the carpets. The Sultan greeted us all again and welcomed me to his province and wished the Polish doctor a happy leave after all the good work for his people in the hospital.

The Scribe then gave a signal and the Resident began saying farewell to the Sultan and thanking him for seeing us, and wished him well and also all his household and counsellors. Then we shook hands again as the Sultan escorted us to the door of the chamber followed by his counsellors, and then an unusual thing happened; it was only later that I found out just how unusual.

The Sultan always leaves his guest at the chamber door, but this time in our honour he came right out to our cars in the courtyard. It was quite impressive to hear and see all his colourful bodyguards bending down shaking both fists at their Sultan and greeting and praising him as he walked through them with us.

On the way back the Resident stopped his car in front of the hospital and we bade our farewells while we went into the hospital to finish the handover.

On my first day of duty in charge of the town, the area and the local hospital, I had a phone call from the Resident. He wanted to see me in his office. My heart almost stopped as I wondered if I had done anything wrong; it was quite something to be called to the 'Queen's Representative' on the first day in the job. Nervously I went to his office at the appointed time. He told me that he wanted to speak to me in extreme confidence and offered me a cigarette and told me not to worry while he got rid of his messenger and police guard! I just could not think what was going to happen and my mind was racing.

The Resident came back, lit a cheroot and again told me to relax, went out again to check that no one was around his office, then he told me the problem that was to confront me. I had to swear over the Bible that I would not let a soul know, not even my wife.

Signed photo of Sultan Abubakar III Sultan of Sokoto for 'the Bearded Doctor'

The Sultan is the religious leader of West African Muslims – some 60 million souls – so a very important influence in West Africa. Each Friday, the holy day, all go to the mosque, and the Sultan leads his followers riding a caparisoned horse, surrounded by his bodyguards, two of whom carry decorative umbrellas which they rotate and twirl to keep him cool.

In recent weeks the Sultan had found that after riding, he had blood running down his right leg, he was terrified that his subjects would see the blood dripping down on the ground. The Sultan had spoken to the Resident who now explained to me the gravity of the situation and the political implications if anything was seen to be wrong with the Sultan.

I agreed to see the Sultan, and the Resident gave me a brief rundown on the protracted greetings that must be used as a form of respect and stressed that things must never be rushed.

The plan was that the Resident would take me down in his car and we would both have an audience, then, after an appropriate time, I was to ask the Sultan if I could see his leg in private. The Resident then rang the Chief Scribe and an appointment was made later that afternoon.

The Resident was quite sure that the Sultan had nothing more than a tropical ulcer on his leg, probably started from getting his calf caught between the stirrup leathers of his saddle. In the car the Resident kept reassuring me as he offered me yet another cigarette.

It was late afternoon and very few people were about so hardly anyone noticed us as we entered the palace. The Chief Scribe met us in the Sultan's compound; unlike the day before there was no sign of the bodyguards, the horses were still tethered and the inevitable goats nosing around and eating the horses' hay, scraggy old chickens clucked about, with the odd one hopping around in the open drains; the palace was deserted.

The Scribe took us to a side entrance where there were several easy chairs, and we sat down, then the Sultan appeared. It was siesta time and he was only wearing his white underrobe, a red fez, with no turban. What a change from his finery the day before, but his face and eyes were so full of dignity and power even without his tulle and elaborately embroidered robes.

The Resident opened the greeting ceremony and after about

twenty minutes the Sultan and I retired to a back room where I could have a look at his leg. The Sultan and I were on our own, my knowledge of Hausa was very limited and here in the inner sanctum we spoke English slowly and simply to each other. The Sultan made me promise not to let anyone know that he understood or spoke English. I promised and in public on many occasions afterwards we spoke just with our eyes.

He drew up his right trouser leg and I saw that he must have been in agony for many weeks. On the inside of his right calf he had a tumour growing the size of a closed fist. It arose from a narrow stalk with a bulbous top. The skin over the top of the tumour had not been able to keep pace with the growth and so the top was completely raw, like a strawberry, no wonder it bled when the Sultan was on horseback. I was shattered, especially after the earlier rundown from the Resident. On superficial examination the tumour did not look cancerous but I had to be sure.

There were three options open. One was to advise the Sultan to go to Kano where there was a qualified surgeon and a theatre team plus all the ancillary services. Then there was our local hospital where we did our best under somewhat primitive conditions; we had a theatre, not air-conditioned, just a couple of table fans, but with excellent nurses who were Southerners. Finally there was the Sultan's palace, the easiest place to keep the utmost secrecy from the population. I put the three proposals to the Sultan and we had a long discussion on the options. The first was out of the question as he could not leave his loyal subjects. The second was possible but he felt that it could not be kept secret, so he decided that I should arrange for the operation to take place in his palace.

Crowds waiting to greet the Sultan

I was to arrange the operation so that his subjects would see him as normal at the mosque on the Friday. His countrymen would be happy and there would be no trouble.

The Sultan then led me back to the room where we had left the Resident, who looked exhausted; he had been sitting there on his own and worried for nearly two hours. We bade our farewells to the Sultan and the Resident drove me back to his office. I explained to him the difficult position, that the Sultan wanted the operation done in his palace, and I described what we needed for an operating room: light, water, drains covered and a soakage pit that would not reveal blood or swabs of cotton wool, so that the household would not suspect anything. It was late that night by the time the Resident and I had formulated a scheme, which he would confirm with the Sultan the following day when he paid his usual administrative call.

I would have a look around the palace to determine the best room to be used as a theatre. To allay any suspicion we had arranged that the Chief Scribe was to take me around every room and soakage pit on the pretext of public health measures to be taken for fly and mosquito control.

I was taken around a household with hundreds of rooms and annexes where no European had ever trod before. Some of the rooms must have been hundreds of years old with walls five to six feet thick, ceilings supported with split palm tree trunks in which small bats nestled. The door portals were clustered with swallow nests and birds swooped up to them, missing us by inches. There were open drains passing through the lanes and corridors and even down the centre of some of the rooms, goats and their dropping were everywhere. We then came across a patio where the Sultan relaxed from the pressure of work, away from his four wives: it was his place. There was a small courtyard where he could sit in the cool of the evening sun with several small bushes to add a bit of green and coolness. In the sitting room there was one central light bulb and a handbasin whose open drain disappeared under the maze of rooms opening out at the back of the palace.

There were two wide windows through the four-foot-thick mud walls and a door that opened out onto the patio and another opening to an inner room with no outside light or door. It was this room that I decided to make into an operating theatre; easily accessible from the Sultan's chamber.

During my inspection with the Scribe I talked about fly breeding and the habits of mosquitoes in sitting on walls and how I would have to get the Public Works Department to renovate some soakage pits and drains to prevent their breeding and to have treated whitewash to paint the interior of the palace to kill the mosquitoes. To allay any suspicion we got the whole interior whitewashed, with paint impregnated with DDT. The Resident must have helped arrange this massive painting procedure as scores of workers were employed to whitewash all the interior walls and ceilings. It took about ten days to complete, during which I paid irregular daily visits to dress and treat the Sultan's leg. I took my car right into the palace grounds and soon no one paid any attention to me. I often visited after dark and I always took a different route to the palace so no one knew what I was up to.

Fortunately for me, at this time there was a police officer's wife expecting a baby, so I could use this as an excuse to take an old but perfectly functional operating table from the hospital. I brought the table home and was helped by my steward to unload it from my car where I left it folded up in the garage. He asked me what this was for so I told him about the policeman's wife expecting 'Spikkin' (baby). The table stayed in my garage for several days until one night I put it back into my estate car and drove around to see the policeman's wife, but did not take the table out. I then took another route and entered the palace. No one paid any attention to me as I took my car through the gates, I then reversed the car to the doorway, arranged with the Scribe (now in the know) who helped me lift in the table into the now whitewashed patio room; no one saw us at this time of night.

Over the past few days, I had taken from the hospital stores old sheets which had been torn up to make suitable dusters. I had these under the front seats, so once the Scribe and I had put up the table I draped it over with my old but clean torn sheets. We then got a couple of carpets and draped them over the whole lot, so anyone passing would not recognise the structure, which now looked like a table or dresser.

I had now the problem of smuggling in the sterile dressing drums, instruments, oxygen cylinders, anaesthetic equipment etc. I did this in much the same way as the theatre table. By now one more person was involved in the secret mission, the Matron of the local hospital. The Sultan kindly consented to her as she now took a major part in the 'operations', even though I had to take her in lying on the floor of my car, behind the front seat!

Next we had to find a way to bring in a surgeon and an anaesthetist without arousing suspicion. Fortunately, medically speaking, there was an accident where I had to deal with seven badly injured people. I was able to deal with six of them myself in the hospital but the seventh had terrible facial injuries, including multiple fractures of the lower jaw. I therefore got in contact with our Orthopaedic Specialist in Kano to come and see this patient and the others whom I had treated. He obligingly flew down to see my patient in the hospital and then as courtesy I took him to visit the Resident, after which we took him to see the Sultan.

I followed the Resident's car with the specialist sitting beside me talking away about this and that; we overtook a couple of unladen donkeys and passed the hospital. Entering the town everyone was waving to us. I thought it was just their recognition of the specialist in my car, but on our arrival at the palace courtyard all the Sultan's bodyguards began pointing at the car and laughing: I had hooked up a donkey's empty pannier on my nearside bumper.

A huge joke for all, especially the guards and the Sultan.

We left the Sultan and I followed the Administrator back to his office where we told the specialist our problem. We arranged that he would return in a week's time to do the operation on a Friday after mosque.

The specialist would come back to visit the cases that I had in the hospital and would then operate; he had to take my word regarding the diagnosis and size of the tumour as he had not seen it! The Resident suggested a Friday for the operation as the Sultan could go to the mosque and with any luck would be at the mosque the following Friday, so even if the news leaked, the people would be happy to see their leader at prayers. Now the problem was to arrange an anaesthetist; by now the Director of Medical Services (DMS) had been informed by the Governor, and by a strange coincidence he arrived at the Rest House on the Thursday night to see some of my accident cases.

On the appointed Friday both the specialist and the DMS visited the hospital early and reviewed the patients; we did our courtesy calls to the Resident and then we all went to the palace and had our usual audience with the Sultan and his counsellors. We all left, and apart from the patient and the Chief Scribe no one knew what was going to happen.

The plan was that we return to operate in the afternoon, the hottest time of day, when everyone was resting after mosque. I could drive in with the specialist and the DMS and no one would take much notice. To my horror the DMS decided to be the assistant to the specialist and that I had to give the Sultan the anaesthetic!

The Matron would call at the palace about half an hour after we intended to operate. She had been in several times before arranging the layout of the 'theatre', the gown drum, buckets, rubber gloves etc.

The operation took about twenty-five minutes, purely under Pentothal intravenous anaesthetic, and everything went off extremely well, with no complications.

The tumour was the size of an orange or tennis ball and had grown out of his calf from a narrow, one-inch stalk, with its surface denuded of skin. It was not a cancerous growth, confirmed about six weeks later after it had been flown to England for a pathology report.

After we cleaned up the theatre the Sultan was waking up and we carried him onto a couch into the inner room where the Chief Scribe was assigned to stay with him.

All the medics and Matron retired to the Residency where, after hearing from us, the Resident got onto the hot scramble line to the Governor to say all was well; the Governor in turn contacted Her Majesty's Foreign Secretary in London, all within a matter of minutes.

On the following Friday the wound on the Sultan's leg was almost healed; I bandaged it well and put on plenty of cotton wool padding. The Sultan then proudly rode his horse to the mosque with no fear or pain.

Mike and the Sultan

The Sultan in his car

Daga Abubakar, Sarki Musulmi
Zuwa ga Aboki, Doctor Hums

Gaisuwa da tambaya lafiyarka
Bayan Wannan Dalili Wannan
takarda Sabada ni naiyana —
maka godiyata akan Himmarka
ta taimako Wanda kayi gareni
ni kai na da kuma Syali na,
Hakika Kayi matukar godiya
da wahalai da ka dauka ta zowa gidana
kai da mai taimakonka Sister
Bazani mancewa da ku ba har Abada
ko da lafiya muka Socai. Balle En —
chiwo ya Abkn!!!

Bllah ne ya kaddaro lafrya da chiwo
kuma yace a nemi Magani, Sabada —
Himmarka chiwo ya gudu bisaga yanda
Bllah mungode Allah shibanu lafiya da
Zama lafiya Amin

Ka Ida godiyata ga Sister da Balarabe

I thank you Likita maigeme.

Letter from the Sultan to 'Likita Maigeme', the Bearded Doctor

Translation of letter from the Sultan to 'the Bearded Doctor'

From Abubakar, Sultan of Sokoto, to his friend Doctor Holmes

Greetings, I am writing this letter to express my thanks for the enthusiasm you have shown in helping me and my family.

Certainly I am very grateful indeed for the trouble you have taken in coming to my house, both you and your assistant, the Nursing Sister.

I shall not forget you for ever even in our healthy state, much less therefore in the state of illness!

Both health and illness are ordained by Allah and He instructs people to seek for medicine. It is due to your enthusiasm that the illness disappeared by the will of Allah. We thank you very much and pray that we continue to be in a healthy state.

Please take my greetings and thanks to the Nursing Sister as well as Balaraba.

I thank you the doctor, the bearded.

20.
LEAVING FOR GOOD

The train, we were told, should arrive at half past two in the morning, but in those days railway communications were not all that good. We only knew for sure that a train was coming when it reached a station or so further up the line. When this happened, we usually had about half an hour to be ready with our luggage to board at the station platform.

We had been to a farewell party the evening before, but left early to get some sleep.

It was now two-thirty am, cold and damp, not quite drizzling, but wet and uncomfortable, and I drove down to the station to enquire when the Lagos train was due. There had been no reports of it in any of the stations north of us, so I went back to bed and catnapped for another hour, then down again to the station. There was still no news, but this time there was no point in going to bed again, so I stayed around the station talking to friends who had come to see us off.

The kindly stationmaster then came to tell me that the train would be arriving in another hour, so back I went to find my wife and family still blissfully asleep. Half-asleep they got dressed, packed toiletries into cases and we drove back to the station.

It was still dark and the morning mist lay heavily round the lights as the train came in. I gave the stationmaster my reservation ticket for our booked compartment and he tried frantically to find it. All we could see when he showed us our compartment was the most enormous lady, whose legs were hanging over the upper berth and whose huge breasts were cupped in a giant red brassiere. There was no way we could all fit in this compartment and so we were forced to retreat hastily to the station. As dawn was breaking, we drove back to the Rest House we had just vacated, only to find it was now shut.

Kind friends gave us breakfast and then drove us to Lagos where we said goodbye for the very last time.

THE END

21.
A MATTER OF PRINCIPLE

Epilogue by Ruth Holmes

We had no idea our leaving would be so abrupt, though we had been troubled for some weeks about the open animosity between the Northerners and the Southerners. In the north, the Hausa and Fulani and others were mainly Muslim, and in the south were the Yoruba, Igbo and Ibibio. We civil servants, employed as teachers, doctors, engineers and so on, were being gradually brought into the controversy. Mary Crawford, the Matron of the local hospital and a good friend, had been accused in a newspaper of favouring Southerners in an examination she had been overseeing. Mary was noted for her integrity in such things and was really troubled about the accusation.

I had recently sat on the sofa at the Residency in Sokoto, next to my husband, with the Sardauna of Sokoto on his other side. My husband had asked how he would be able to run a hospital with staff who had failed their examinations. The Sardauna replied in a measured and reasonable tone of voice, "Well, Doctor Holmes, that is what you will have to do. Or you will have to leave us."

Michael had by now long experience of the strict steps that had to be taken in the hospitals before any member of staff could be sacked. When he discovered that the manager of a hospital under his charge had been guilty of very serious misconduct, Michael was as meticulous as ever in how he went about things. He sent the three warning notices that were required and ensured there was nothing that could be used to discredit the charge, so that the authorities could not overlook the matter. The manager was a Northerner. Michael did not usually discuss matters such as dismissal with me, but this time he felt worried about the new policy. Another doctor in government service that we knew well had been having difficulties with the results of this policy but had decided to carry on for a while and see how long this state of affairs would last.

Brass plate – for Mr and Mrs M. Ma. Holmes, Medical Officer Northern Nigeria, from Mr and Mrs M.E. Iso, Calabar, 1958

We discussed the situation at length. We knew we would not carry on should the charge against the hospital manager fail to remove him. Michael, though anxious, was optimistic and honestly felt the authorities would have no option other than to remove the manager. Furthermore, Dr Dikko, a high-ranking Indian doctor, whom Michael liked and respected, would be heading the committee.

The meeting took place and I can see to this day the relief on Michael's face as he told me the result: the verdict was guilty and the manager was to be removed from his post. We were delighted with this fair play, as we saw it.

A week or so later Michael returned with very bad news. The manager was to be reinstated; this was the request of the Emir to whom he was related. The term 'brother' was often used loosely, but in this case I believe it really was a blood relationship. I am not sure whether Michael knew this, but he had not considered that he would be asked to reinstate the man.

An Emir had much power over those he controlled, but Michael had never experienced anything like this type of interference in the medical services, neither working as a medical officer with the Colonial Service, nor afterwards as a civil servant.

We were absolutely shocked, and wasted no time in agreeing Michael's response. He resigned immediately and made immediate hurried preparations for us to travel to Lagos.

At no time did we imagine that there might possibly be a war and it was with very mixed feelings that we boarded an Elder Dempster liner in Lagos for the last time.

Written from:
Commonwealth Relations Office,
Downing Street, S.W.1.

20th January, 1964

Dear Dr Holmes

On your retirement from public service
overseas, the Secretary of State has asked
me to let you know of his appreciation of your
valuable work for the Government and people of
Northern Nigeria since you were first appointed
in 1953.

He sends you his thanks and best wishes
for the future.

Yours sincerely

(N.B.J. Huijsman)
Private Secretary.

Dr. M. McA. Holmes,
    13 Ardenlee Avenue,
        Ravenhill Road,
            Belfast, N.1.

Letter of appreciation from the Secretary of State, 1964

Ruth, Alison and Thomas with the girls of Queen Elizabeth School, Ilorin, 1962. Ilorin was our place of departure

The Bearded Doctor, Michael McAlister Holmes

M McA HOLMES

MB, BCH, BAO, DOBSTRCOG, DTM&H

Dr M McA Holmes, who was senior medical officer with the Commonwealth Development Corporation in Swaziland, has died at the age of 55.

Michael McAlister Holmes was born in 1925 into a Northern Irish medical family.

His father was a surgeon captain in the Royal Navy and a general practitioner at Llandovery, Carmarthenshire, where Michael spent his childhood. Later he went to the Methodist College at Belfast and then graduated from Queen's University in 1950. After house jobs at the Royal Victoria and Royal Maternity hospitals, Belfast, he took the diploma in obstetrics. He spent a short time in general practice and then joined the Colonial Medical Service and went to Northern Nigeria, where he practised for 10 years. Michael was a talented surgeon and an excellent diagnostician, and the challenge of practising medicine in difficult and sometimes primitive conditions was what he enjoyed most. He had a gift for organisation and generated enthusiasm among his patients and colleagues. He was appointed SMO, and, working for the Northern Nigerian Government, was responsible for the medical services of vast and heavily populated areas. As an administrator he had the art of keeping different nationalities and different sections of the community working harmoniously together, and he had seemingly unlimited energy.

After leaving Nigeria in 1963 he tried to settle in practice in Northern Ireland, but he missed the scope of medicine and life in general in Africa. In 1974 he joined a practice at Dar es Salaam, first as a partner and later as principal of the leading practice in the city. He left reluctantly in 1970 when financial restrictions for expatriates became increasingly difficult and worked in Aden for the British Petroleum Oil Company for three years. He returned to his home in County Down and again attempted to settle in Ireland, this time practising in the south. He enjoyed the people and country life, but again felt the pull of Africa, and in 1976 he took up an SMO post with the Commonwealth Development Corporation in North-east Swaziland and was back in his element. He was instrumental in having a complete new clinic and maternity unit built, the latter opening just two months before he died.

With his irrepressible good humour, he had the capacity of doing the unexpected—a feature that his wife and family had long given up trying to control. His warm, friendly, cheerful personality endeared him to his patients, to whom he was dedicated. In his early life he had rowed and played rugby, later polo. He was a good shot, but gave up shooting for the camera, for he had a great love and concern for wild life and conservation. Michael, who had such zest for life, showed great cheerfulness and courage during his long illness. He is survived by his wife Ruth, a son, and a daughter who is a medical student at Cambridge.—JEP.